LONDON

PLACES AND HISTORY

STEWART, TABORI & CHANG
NEW YORK

Text
Chiara Libero

Editing Supervision
Valeria Manferto De Fabianis

Art Director
Patrizia Balocco Lovisetti

Graphic Supervision
Anna Galliani

Translation
Neil Frazer Davenport

1 *Symbols of power are everywhere in London, even in this sculpture on the banks of the Thames.*

2 and 7
The frontispiece of The Illustrated London News, *a 19th-century periodical, provides an image of a wealthy London. Behind this facade lay a very different city: the London described by Dickens and Disraeli.*

3–6 *A view of the City from the Thames. Skyscrapers rise alongside the symbols of political power and religion. The name of the river that divides the city in two derives from the Celtic* teme. *Throughout the long history of London the Thames has been one of the city's principal arteries.*

Published in 1998 and distributed by
Stewart, Tabori & Chang,
a division of U.S. Media Holdings, Inc.
115 West 18th Street, New York, NY 10011

Distributed in Canada by
General Publishing Company Ltd.
30 Lesmill Road
Don Mills, Ontario, M3B 2T6, Canada

Library of Congress Catalog Card
Number: 97-68226

ISBN 1-55670-692-8

Printed in Italy

10 9 8 7 6 5 4 3 2 1

First Edition

CONTENTS

True Cockneys are born within the sound of the bells of St. Mary-le-Bow in the City. Cockneys are the men and women who consider this damp, crowded, lively, and formal capital to be the greatest place on Earth, and who would probably cut off their own right hands rather than forego their warm beer, shepherd's pie, and fish-and-chips. Cockneys use a slang incomprehensible not only to foreigners but also to other Englishmen, a language in constant evolution, based on audacious rhymes and puns. Another Cockney characteristic is solidarity. Cockneys are happy to make a fool of anybody they do not recognize as one of their own. Absolute honesty reigns within the clan, along with a sense of humor and a love of a pint or two and a good song, in the usual pub, with the usual crowd.

Until a few years ago, Cockneys were rigorously white and Anglo-Saxon. Today, however, you are likely to find more Cockneys in the suburbs than in the City: spiralling rents have forced them far from Bow Bells. You might well find an Indian or a Pakistani using Cockney slang and a Jamaican making fools of the white Anglo-Saxons in the markets. Those content to visit the London on an inclusive tour—see it all in three days, with an evening in an "authentic" pub part of the package—will never see that in this immense city saris and turbans are increasingly more common than bowler hats and pinstripes. The non-white, non-Anglo-Saxon population now exceeds 20% of the total population of the city.

The change in London's demographics is not, as many believe, a recent phenomenon. It is the result of a process of immigration that began in the 16th century with the great imperial expansion, when the British Crown exerted power over distant lands from India to the Caribbean. When the empire collapsed, immigration reached unprecedented levels.

The same situation is happening today with Hong Kong citizens, who have every right to enter the motherland and to form integrated yet distinct communities with their own characteristics. The Cockneys have had to learn to live with bright costumes, carnival celebrations, and richly perfumed markets.

Eastern spices are nothing new to British cooking, and tea has long been adopted as a Great British emblem. In modern-day London, it is often easier to find exotic delicacies than English roast beef.

This does not mean that the city has been transformed into a Jamaican market, but it is indicative of how a place that in the collective imagination is formal and restrained is able to accept and exploit even radical changes. The empire and its global role as arbiter having been lost—the duties being handed over to

8 top
The winged figure of Victory on the hood of a Rolls-Royce in London. Among the various cars in Queen Elizabeth's stable is an extraordinary brown and black Phantom VI, the largest built in the past 50 years, with the rear section of the upper body in glass to allow her subjects to see the sovereign. The queen has replaced the internal bar with a sophisticated stereo system that plays military marches.

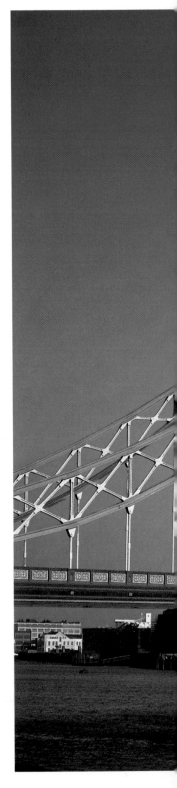

8–9 *Tower Bridge rarely has to be opened to allow the passage of river traffic. The structure attracts thousands of visitors from all over the world. Since 1982, tourists have been able to cross the river on a walkway suspended above the river*

9 top
Elegantly dressed ladies and gentlemen are often encountered in London's streets.

10 top and 10–11
A bright red double-decker bus, one of London's best-known symbols. The old buses, with rear platforms and spiral staircases, are gradually being replaced by new models that lack one of the city's most characteristic figures: the bus conductor who asks passengers' destinations, takes their fares, and issues tickets. Today, the driver is responsible for these duties. A trip on the top deck of a double-decker bus is still one of the most enjoyable parts of a stay in London.

Washington and New York—London, and the rest of Great Britain, has experienced long periods of economic and social crisis.

What has in part saved London is language: the English of London is by no means the same as the English spoken on the other side of the Atlantic. Great Britain's language-school business is enormous. Thousands of students arrive each year from Europe, Asia, and Africa. They all need lodgings, they all eat in the fast-food restaurants, and they all spend money in the schools for foreigners. The most diligent students spend their weekends in museums, the night owls among them frequent the discothèques, and virtually all of them return home with the idea that London is, potentially, the world's greatest city.

While it might not be as beautiful as Rome or Paris, as intriguing as Prague, or as outrageous as New York, London really is a fascinating place in which to live.

11 top
A solitary carriage heading for Buckingham Palace. Alongside aristocratic London, still clinging to its ancient traditions, there is another city all bustle and modernity.

11 bottom
A member of the Queen's Life Guards at the Tower of London. The various guards regiments play a fundamental role in the complex ceremonies that punctuate the daily routines of the city's great monuments. At the Tower of London, the Ceremony of the Keys is performed each evening to close the gates after the last "stranger" has left.

During the 1960s, fashion and music gave rise to a modern myth that still survives in London. The city has exported throughout the world lifestyles, clothes, music, and the illusion that the city is there for the taking, just by walking down Oxford Street dressed in a miniskirt. The fact that Londoners who were more than 25 years old during the '60s looked askance at the multicolored crowd convinced of their power to change the world with love and peace is lost.

12 top
Big Ben is not, as many believe, the name of the bell tower of the Houses of Parliament, but of the great 14-ton bell that tolls the hours. The nickname comes from Sir Benjamin Hall, who was Commissioner of Works when the bell was hung in 1858. Big Ben is the second bell to be hung in tower (the first was cracked during trials). The clock is the largest in the United Kingdom, and even in the digital age, its accuracy is proverbial.

The blows to the economy and the welfare state sustained during the Thatcher years diminished the allure of the 1960s to some extent, but it has failed to dim the appeal of the city in the eyes of those who love her. London is many experiences: evenings in the pubs; afternoons in the Victoria and Albert Museum library handling precious manuscripts under the paternal gaze of the guard; Sunday-morning strolls through the Regent's Park rose garden; Harrods' sales; the market at Brixton with its mysterious fruits and magical herbs; days browsing in bookshops in search of the ghost of Edith Sitwell or in hunting down an elusive art book; a greeting to Peter Pan and another to Boadicea.

The families that provide lodgings for students and live in any of the myriad suburban outposts linked by the underground system occasionally visit the city center, rarely go to the West End theaters, and inhabit a microcosm centered around a tube station, a church—or synagogue, mosque, temple, or chapel—a post office, and a main road with shops and banks. They are far removed from the town planners' earnest discussions of the Docklands renaissance, the sociologists' treatises on the punks, Soho's red-light district, and the connoisseurs' arguments over the influence of ethnic cooking on Old English cuisine. They have very little in common with the Mayfair aristocracy and the Bond Street shops, with the gentlemen's clubs or the affairs of the city. And yet they, too, are Londoners.

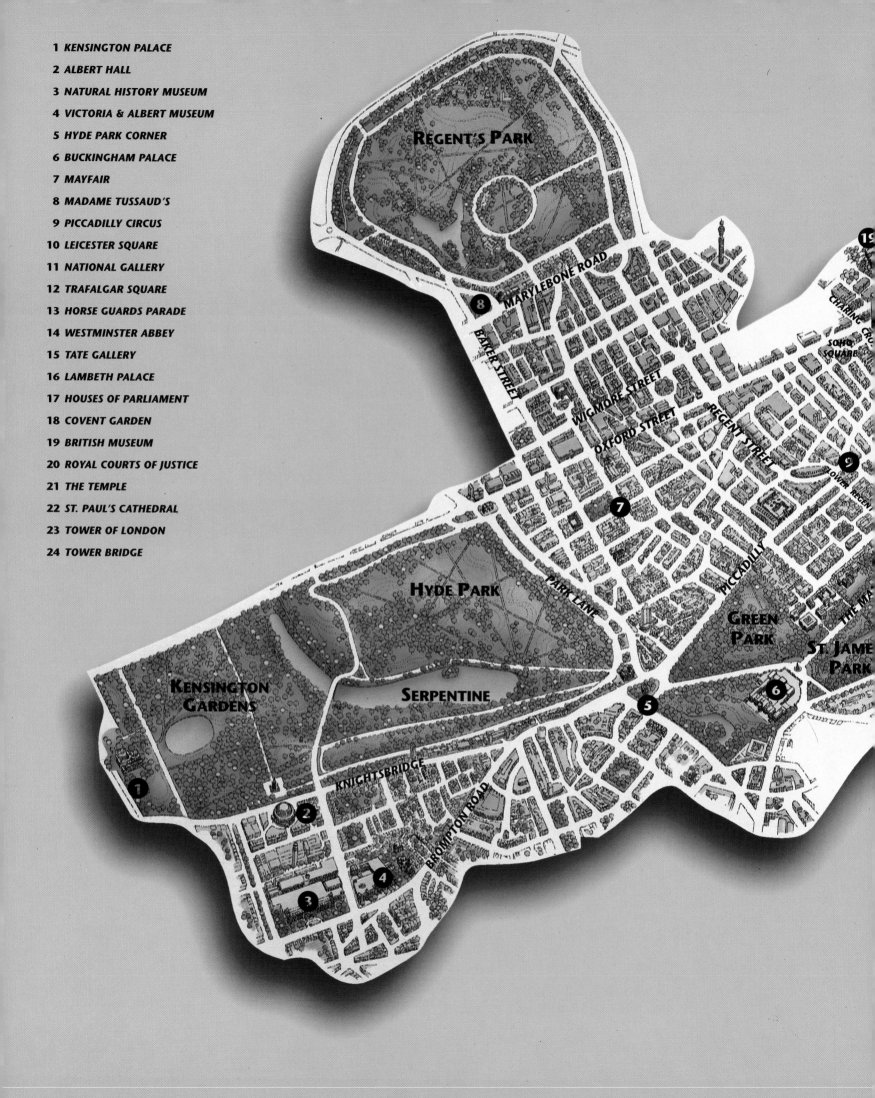

HIGH HOLBORN

FLEET STREET

QUEEN VICTORIA ST.

RIVER THAMES

LONDON BRIDGE

STRAND

EMBANKMENT

VICTORIA

WHITEHALL

WESTMINSTER BRIDGE

Westminster, the seat of parliament.

Piccadilly Circus.

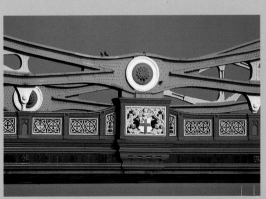

London Bridge.

20–21 *A map of Roman London. The name probably derived from the Celtic term* Llyn-din, *which means "fortress near the lake." The original settlement consisted of wooden huts principally used to house livestock. The choice of site on which to found the city was apparently dictated by the fact that here the river could be easily forded and access to the sea was close by. Quays allowed ships for the transport of troops and goods to be moored. The map reproduced here shows the grid pattern typical of Roman cities, with streets intersecting at right angles and a surrounding wall. Important roads led out from the center to other Roman cities established on the island: the present-day Bath, Colchester, York, Chester, Exeter, and Canterbury.*

L ondon has Roman roots. Before the conquest of the island, Londinium was probably a Celtic village, Llyn-din. The Romans' choice of site was virtually inevitable because here the Thames was easily fordable and the vicinity of the sea eased the problems of trade and communications with the rest of the empire. Londinium was a prosperous and extensive settlement by the standards of the day, with temples, a basilica, workshops, and a necropolis.

Roman domination suffered a severe setback because of the efforts of one remarkable woman, Boadicea, the queen of the Iceni. Boadicea, the widow of King Prasutagus, attempted to accede to her husband's throne. The Romans, however, made it quite clear that her minor kingdom was only important as land to be appropriated. This they did with such arrogance that Boadicea rallied her troops and led a revolt. The Romans eventually quelled the uprising, but the fearless queen had the satisfaction of sacking the wooden Roman village located more or less where London Bridge stands today.

Londinium was reconstructed, and the new town was built around a wooden bridge, with warehouses for goods, homes, and a temple dedicated to Mithras. The remains of Roman walls are not far from the Tower of London, and entire mosaics from the period have been discovered in the City, together with relics that can be admired in the British Museum and the Museum of London.

London's most important streets follow the routes of the great Roman roads: Oxford Street leads to the West, the long Mile End Road to the East, and Old Kent Road to the South. Under the Emperor Augustus, London developed into a commercial and administrative jewel, but the city's position was not to last.

20 top
This small statue, found in the waters of the Thames, depicts an Egyptian divinity adopted by the Romans and imported into their lands of conquest.

20 bottom
Boadicea, the queen of the Iceni, led a rebellion against the Roman invaders and sacked the city of Londinium.
The illustration is taken from a work by Meyrick and Smith dedicated to the customs of the inhabitants of the British Isles (1815).

21 top
A bronze bust of
Hadrian, found in
the Thames, and a
coin minted during
his reign bear witness
to the success of the
Roman expeditions
after the conquest of
Britain by Julius
Caesar in 55 and 54
BC. Hadrian
sponsored the
construction of the
"vallum" (known as
Hadrian's Wall), the
moat around the
empire designed to
protect it from
marauding tribes.

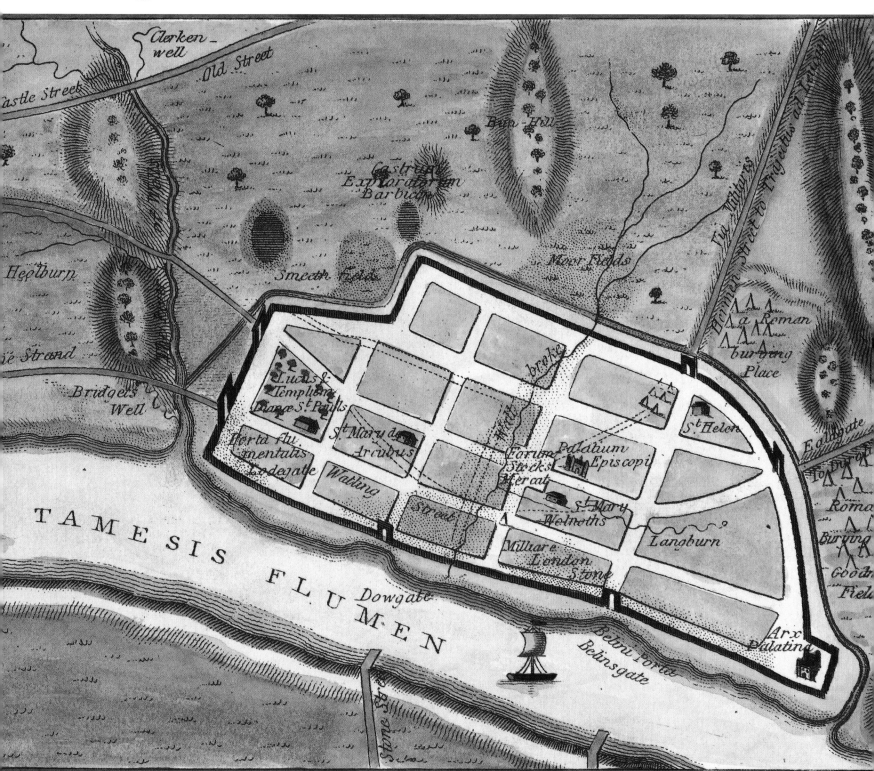

K. EDWARD the CONFESSOR.

The decline began in AD 410, not only for Londinium, but for all Roman Britain. After the imperial capital was obliged to recall its garrisons to the continental mainland to defend itself against the Germanic hordes, the colony, left to its own devices, began to decay.

During the dark ages, the city fell into the hands of the Saxons

and acquired a certain importance at least in part because of the spread of Christianity. At the end of the 6th century, when Pope Gregory I appointed the future St. Augustine as archbishop of Canterbury, London was defined by the Venerable Bede as "the market of the world." It was soon to be given a cathedral, St. Paul's, and became a see in 604. But London was still a provincial settlement confined by the borders established by the Romans.

A great urban expansion began in 1042 with the accession to throne of Edward the Confessor, the last Saxon king. Edward transferred the royal seat to a monastery on Thorney Island, Westminster Abbey, where all his successors were to be crowned.

23 top
An episode in the life of Hengist, the Anglo-Saxon leader who is said to have colonized the kingdom of Kent.

23 bottom left
A miniature executed in the Benedictine San Gallo Monastery depicting St. Gregory the Great, who sent a group of monks to Britain. The group was headed by Augustine, the future archbishop of Canterbury.

23 bottom right
Ethelbert, the king of Kent and the author of the first Anglo-Saxon legal code, was baptized by St. Augustine.

24 top
The Queen Matilda Tapestry, in the Bayeux Museum, depicts the Norman conquest of England in 58 scenes. The scene on the left portrays William the Conqueror, and the one on the right shows the sovereign and his fleet attacking Dinan on the French coast.

24–25 *The French infantry repelling the Norman attack. This episode bears little resemblance to the real events: On October 14, 1066, the infantry could do little to stop the Norman cavalry. William the Conqueror's political and military skills had been revealed in his homeland, where, at a very young age, he succeeded in putting down a baronial rebellion and in gaining the protection and support of the Church.*

25 top
In a contemporary miniature, the Battle of Hastings (1066), the final phase of William the Conqueror's victorious campaign to unite the kingdoms of Normandy and England under his rule. During the battle, William defeated the English forces led by Harold of Wessex. To legitimize his operation, William carried with him the vexillum sancti Petri, a sacred banner sent to him by the Pope. With this, he could claim the protection and support of the Holy See, of which he declared himself a servant.

25 bottom
William's victory in the Battle of Hastings was celebrated with a banquet, illustrated in one of the scenes of the Queen Matilda Tapestry, and by the crowning of William on December 25, 1066, at Westminster Abbey.

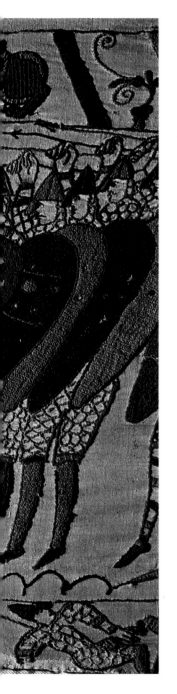

The arrival of the Normans and the reign of William the Conqueror increased the importance of the western area of London. William boosted urban development with the construction of a powerful fortress, the White Tower that is now part of the Tower of London, and he provided the city with a privileged administrative structure with an elected mayor flanked by counts.

Expansion along the right bank of the Thames began with the construction of the stone London Bridge, and trade prospered in the city. Goods arrived via the river, and bartering took place in the narrow, winding streets that replaced the regular Roman plan and are still a characteristic feature of the oldest part of the city. The new St. Paul's Cathedral was London's religious center and oversaw numerous parish churches.

Trading colonies from the continent were established in the city, with groups of Danes, Dutchmen, Italians, and Germans. London also housed Jewish bankers, but they were stripped of their goods in the late 18th century and thrown out of the city. In 1215, the Magna Carta was signed by King John; the document guaranteed the guilds' great municipal autonomy: "the city of London shall retain all its ancient liberties and customs."

27 *This miniature, taken from a 15th-century book, shows a view of London with the White Tower. The tower was completed in 1097 under the aegis of William the Conqueror and is the central keep of the Tower of London. Since Norman times it has been used variously as a royal zoo, a storehouse, and a prison. Today, the appearance of the building reflects the modifications made by the architect Christopher Wren in the 18th century. On the ground floor is the "Little Ease," an extremely small, windowless cell in which the worst criminals were detained. The spiral staircase in the northeast turret rises in a counterclockwise direction to allow defenders to use their swords in their right hands.*

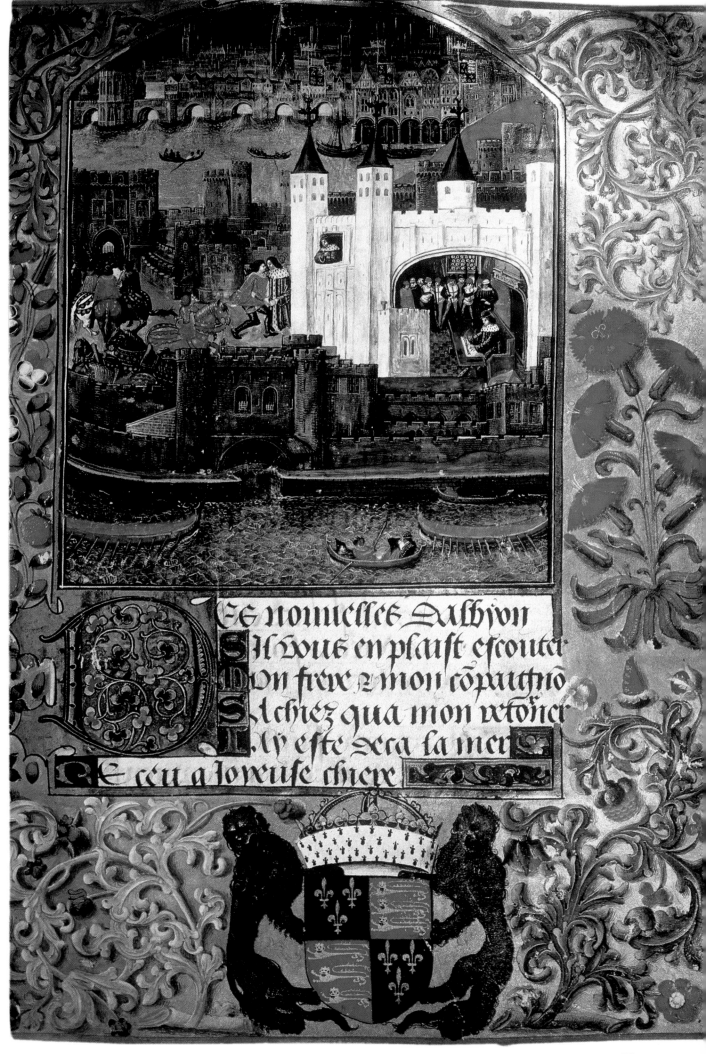

28 top
A dramatic illustration of the plague that ravaged Europe, including London, in 1348.

28 bottom
The assassination of Wat Tyler, the leader of the Peasants' Revolt in a miniature taken from the Chronicle of English History *from the 15th century. The episode aroused the wrath of Richard II.*

28 center
In 1381, a mob marched on London to protest the taxes imposed to finance the Hundred Years' War. This miniature shows Richard II sailing on the Thames to meet the rebels at Rotherhithe.

In 1348, London's prosperity was dealt a severe blow. Plague fell upon the city in an era in which London was home to more than 50,000 people and wealth was in the hands of those controlling trade. There was little incentive for expansion in the city during the plague.

A few decades later, in 1381, the Peasants' Revolt saw an uprising by underprivileged citizens who had been taxed to pay for the Hundred Years' War with France and the various military offensives that England undertook on the continent. The rebellion was short-lived, but it posed a serious threat to the status

quo and endangered the safety of the archbishop.

Feudal order was restored after the uprising, and the increasingly powerful merchants celebrated their position of absolute economic privilege with the construction of the Guildhall in 1440. This symbol of mercantile power still exists and still features in the ceremony of the "silent exchange," in which the Lord Mayor of London receives the symbols of his office.

29 *The revolt of 1381 gave rise to numerous episodes that inflamed the popular spirit, including the preaching of John Ball (top picture) and the killing of the archbishop of Canterbury (bottom picture). The young king did all he could to restore peace, negotiating with the rebels and promising concessions. But every initiative he made was nullified by the intervention of parliament. With his prestige declining, Richard II attempted a coup d'état but was defeated by the aristocracy led by Thomas of Gloucester.*

vant ce vint le ven
dredp au matin ce
peuple qui estoit
logie en la place Sainte Kathe
rine xcvant la tour du chastel

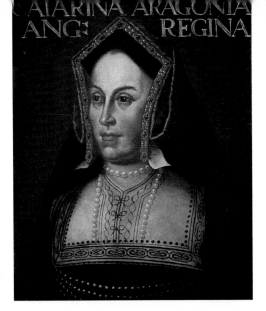

30 top
*Catherine of Aragon,
(left) and Anne
Boleyn (right) were the
first two wives of
Henry VIII.*

30 center
*The Anglican
reformation led to the
English crown's break
with the Church of
Rome.*

30 bottom
*Henry VIII earned a
place in history*

*because of his bloody
marital affairs. After
Catherine of Aragon
and Anne Boleyn, he
married Jane Seymour,
Anne of Cleves,
Catherine Howard,
and Catherine Parr.*

30–31 *Early in his
reign, Henry VIII (here
with Archbishop
Sherbourne) assumed
anti-Lutheran positions
and was appointed
Defender of the Faith by
the Pope.*

Despite the increase in its population, London remained a medieval city, still largely confined within the Roman walls. The peasants who arrived from the countryside were forced to live in miserable conditions, and extending the city limits became a pressing concern. At last the city center was allowed to expand, and a form of local government was established. A king, followed by an extraordinary queen, determined the city's future layout: London and England's golden age was marked by the reigns of Henry VIII and his daughter Elizabeth I.

Henry VIII is considered by many historians and town planners to be the true founder of modern London. The reform of 1536 that

formalized England's secession from the Church of Rome and the creation of the Church of England was also the occasion of an important urban transformation. The dissolution of the monasteries made available a great deal of land and property that the sovereign distributed as gifts and sold to his favorites and supporters. London thus began to expand beyond the confines of the City and Westminster, and many religious buildings were converted into hospices, orphanages, refuges for senior citizens, and prisons.

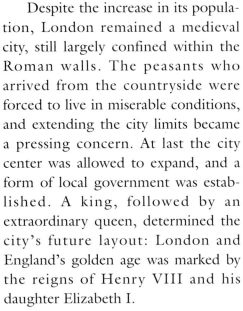

31 top left
Martin Luther, in a portrait by Lucas Cranach, was principally responsible for the secession of the western church.

31 top right
Henry VIII's petition for divorce from his first wife, Catherine of Aragon.

32 *Two contemporary prints of the Tower of London, a veritable citadel composed of a number of buildings. The structure was begun by Gundulf, bishop of Rochester, after the Battle of Hastings and was intended to be a military fortress on a strategic site on the banks of the river just outside the city walls. In the center is the White Tower, the ancient nucleus. The Tower of London was used as a royal palace until the reign of James I because its architectural features made it extremely secure. Today, the Tower houses the Crown Jewels and one of the world's most spectacular armories. According to various legends, numerous ghosts, the spirits of those executed during its long history, roam the Tower.*

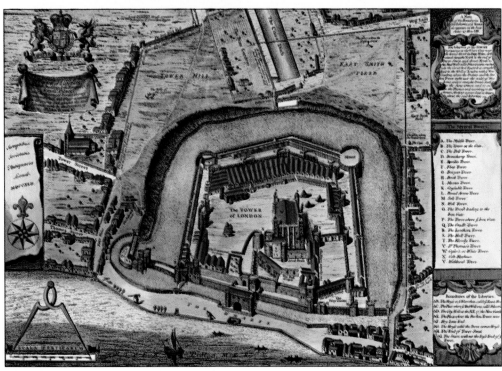

32–33 *A map of London from the 16th century. The area to the south of the Thames was almost completely undeveloped. On the right is the imposing bulk of the Tower of London, just past London Bridge and the City, the oldest part of the metropolis.*

33 top left
The customshouse in a watercolor by Bartholomew Howlett from 1663. Three years later, the complex was destroyed, together with much of the city, in the Great Fire of London.

33 top right
London Bridge in the era of Elizabeth I. In 1967, the old bridge was sold to an American company for $2.5 million. It was then dismantled and rebuilt, brick by brick, in Arizona.

LONDINVM FERACISSIMI AN GLIAE REGNI METROPOLIS

THE TOWRE

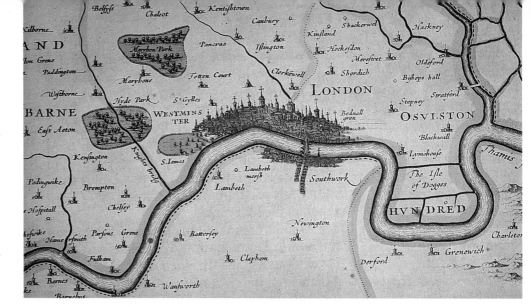

34 top

A map of London in 1640, taken from the Atlas Novus. During the reign of Elizabeth I, the population of the city increased from 50,000 to more than 200,000.

34 center

Elizabeth I, in a celebrated portrait by Marcus Geeraerts the Younger. The queen, who came to the throne in 1558, at 27 years of age, governed with energy and determination, and the era identified with her name was characterized by the presence of great artists and illustrious writers.

34 bottom

Oliver Cromwell was proclaimed Lord Protector in 1653 in Westminster Hall, the same place where Charles I had been sentenced to death.

The work continued after Elizabeth I's accession to the throne, and by the early 17th century, London was composed of three distinct parts: the old City, which had retained its role as an economic and trading center and also contained the homes of the citizens; Westminster, which along with the St. James estate (the royal deer park) was the seat of political power; and the brand-new quarter of Southwark, which was built on land confiscated from the church and became a modern "industrial zone."

Between 1530 and 1600, the population within London's walls numbered 75,000, but no less than 150,000 people lived in the suburbs, where silk, glass, and ceramics industries flourished. Great commercial monopolies such as the Moscow, Levant, and East India companies were also created.

This was the era of Shakespeare, who, to sidestep a mayoral edict prohibiting theatrical productions in the city, sought out a suitable site to the south. The Globe, one of the world's most celebrated theaters was built at the southern end of London Bridge.

The building of Covent Garden, initiated by the duke of Bedford, followed shortly afterward. The city's new section had a regular street plan, unlike the labyrinthine old City; buildings echoing the styles of Renaissance Italy; open spaces; and quarters located around a square with areas dedicated to commerce, religion, and society. The piazzas developed in the 17th century—Leicester Square, Soho Square, and St. James's Square—can still be seen today. The architect who had the greatest influence on the city's new direction was Inigo Jones, a devotee of Andrea Palladio and the author of the design for the Covent Garden complex.

35 top
William Shakespeare was born in Stratford-upon-Avon and arrived in London at the end of the 16th century.

35 bottom left
Inigo Jones in a portrait by Dobson. Jones returned to England in 1605 after a stay in Denmark and began to work for Queen Anne and King James I. Seven of his works survive to bear witness to his love of Italian art and architecture.

35 bottom right
The Globe Theatre in a watercolor by James Stowe. Because the mayor and the city council had banned theatrical performances from the city, the new theater was built on the south bank of the Thames.

Two great tragedies were responsible for further developments in the city's urban planning. In 1664, a plague swept the city (resulting in the death of about 100,000 inhabitants), followed two years later by a devastating fire that swept away much of London. The flames destroyed 13,000 buildings and 87 churches.

The Great Fire of London proved to be a remarkable opportunity for architect Sir Christopher Wren, the General Superintendent to the Crown, who was responsible for reconstructing the city. Wren had

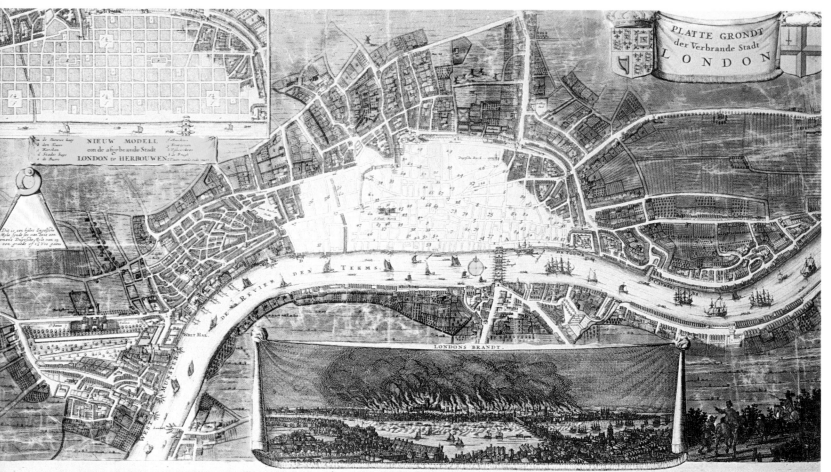

36 top
A print taken from a mid-17th-century frontispiece of a book describing the tragedy of the plague that struck the city and the surrounding area. The illustration shows the dead being given a decent burial in London and being thrown into a common grave in the countryside.

36 bottom
London and the Great Fire of 1666, which started in a baker's shop in Pudding Lane. The fire destroyed 13,000 houses and 87 parish churches.

37 left
Sir Christopher Wren, in a portrait by John Closterman. The architect prepared grandiose designs intended to give the center of London a more solemn atmosphere, but his ideas were adopted only in part.

37 top right
Christopher Wren's original design for St. Paul's Cathedral. The great dome was intended to rise above all other buildings. The building was rightly considered to be the architect's masterpiece and was built on a site that had been sacred to Londoners since the 7th century.

37 bottom right
Mansion House, the official residence of the Lord Mayor of London, was designed by George Dance.

grandiose ideas and immediately began planning a very different city with airy, spacious squares, and broad avenues. Unfortunately, Wren was limited by British traditionalism and the need to rebuild quickly. But he was commissioned to rebuild 51 churches, first and foremost among which was his masterpiece, the new St. Paul's.

The urgency of the rebuilding program led to an expansion that in turn encouraged the construction of buildings in the West End, new bridges over the Thames—Westminster, Blackfriars, Battersea—and new suburbs on the south bank. The creation of the Bank of England in 1694 provided the wealthy bourgeois merchants with a formidable instrument. Those with means fled the overcrowding of the East End, and new working-class quarters were created.

38–39 A contemporary print of Leicester Square in 1751. The harmonious geometry of the square is unrecognizable today, because the square is cluttered with nightclubs and young people looking for entertainment. The transformation took place in 1874, when a speculator decided to alter the 18th-century plan that had featured a large garden surrounded by railings.

39 top A panoramic view of London in 1750. London Bridge and the dome of St. Paul's Cathedral are clearly visible. The West End began to expand during this period, and New Road, extending the Oxford Street route northward, was completed. The building of the road led to further expansion of the city. In the same era, the Bloomsbury quarter was created, and the numerous villages that had sprung up around the old nucleus began to be joined together.

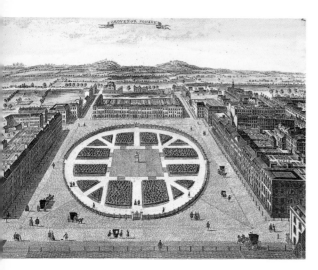

By the 18th century, London had about 750,000 inhabitants. Immigrants arrived from Ireland and Europe, and Great Britain assumed a leading role in global trade, dominating the seas and establishing colonies. Thus began the golden age of London architecture, financed by mercantile trade, with residential quarters constructed on the great estates of influential Whig and Tory families: Hanover Square, Bedford Square, Russell Square.

The city center was embellished with sublime architectural crescents such as those designed by John Nash. A typical example is Regent Street, which links the elegant, exclusive St. James's area with the Regent's Park development. Nash was also responsible for initiating work on what was to become Trafalgar Square and for beginning Buckingham Palace. Under his influence, great public buildings, such as the National Gallery, the British Museum, and the arch at Hyde Park Corner, were constructed in the neoclassical style.

This was the London in which Thackeray set his *Vanity Fair*, a lively city full of opportunity for those like Becky Sharpe, who had their wits about them, and a complete contrast to the somnolent countryside.

38 top
An engraving showing Buckingham Palace as it appeared early in the 18th century. At that time, the building belonged to John Sheffield, the duke of Buckingham, who was married to the daughter of James II. The brick edifice featured wings linked to the central block by colonnades.

38 bottom
Grosvenor Square, in the heart of Mayfair, was, like many other developments, such as Hanover Square, Piccadilly, and Berkeley Square, built as a result of property speculation that followed the Great Fire and continued throughout the 18th century.

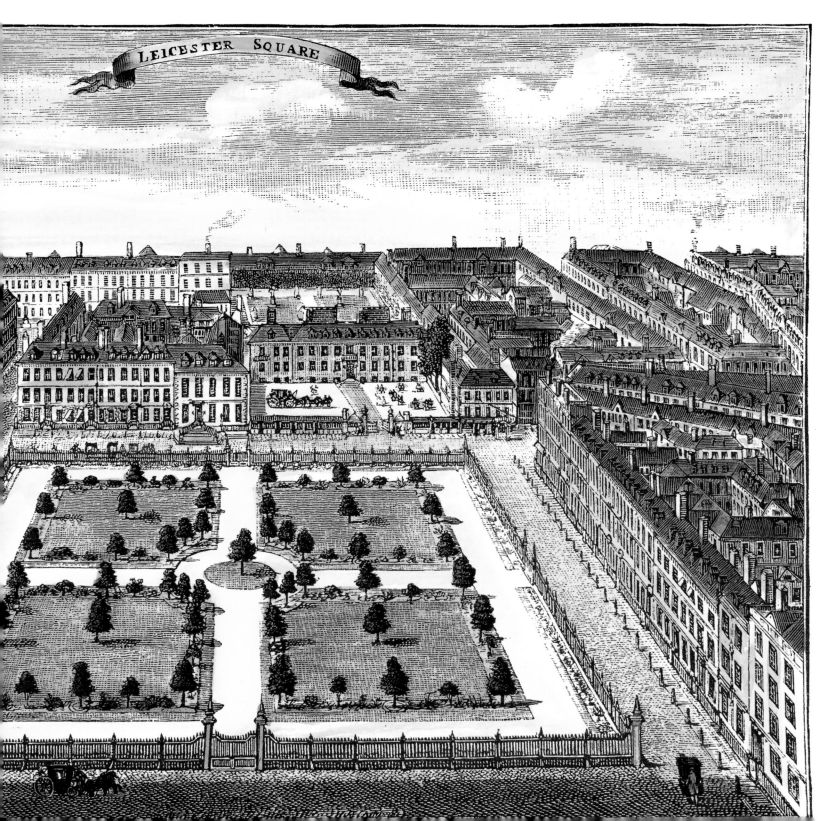

40 top left
The commercial importance of the city increased because of its trading relations with the rest of the world, and by the end of the century, it was calculated that the docks extended for almost 60 miles. Today, merchant ships no longer arrive in the Pool of London, but the Docklands revival project is bringing the area back to life.

40 bottom left
In 1760, Covent Garden Market belonged, as it still does today, to the duke of Bedford. This was the first London district to be built according to a town plan. Until 1974, the area housed the wholesale fruit, vegetable, and flower markets. In the background is the Church of St. Paul, which was designed by Inigo Jones in the "Greek" style and adopted as the actors' church. Today, the area is a lively agglomeration of shops, stalls, and small antiques shops.

40 right
A print of Ludgate Hill in the 19th century. In that era the residential areas of the City were being replaced by office buildings, and the inhabitants were evicted. The arrival of the railways in the heart of the city exacerbated the situation. The viaducts penetrated a maze of busy, narrow streets strewn with straw, where workers, housewives, and hawkers all jostled for space among the carriages and omnibuses.

41 A painting by Canaletto showing the procession of the Knights of the Order of the Bath in front of Westminster Abbey. The abbey is a splendid example of Gothic architecture and was consecrated in 1269. Subsequently, it was subjected to a series of modifications while still remaining one of the symbols of the British Crown.

Wealth and development were not evident throughout London, however. If there were areas in which luxury appeared to be the norm, there were also hivelike workers' districts constructed to house the great wave of labor attracted by the nascent industrial revolution. In 1821, after a flood of immigrants, there were 1,140,000 Londoners, a veritable army of people.

London was the world's financial capital, and its stock exchange determined the fluctuations in the prices of materials. The needs of industry affected the urban structure, and the city expanded exponentially; the inhabitants of the City, which was now overrun by offices, commercial buildings, and warehouses, were obliged to abandon their old homes. To allow both blue- and white-collar workers to reach their workplaces, a railway network was constructed. Although it was very advanced for its era, it left great scars in the historic heart of London. A contemporary print reveals what life must have been like in the City: below the Ludgate Hill viaduct, in view of the dome of St. Paul's, wagons, carts, potato sellers, gentlemen in top hats, and commoners swarm. The creation of the artificial dock basins permanently changed the districts lining the banks of the Thames.

42–43 *London between the 17th and 18th centuries. The painting, by Jan Griffier, hangs in the Sabauda Gallery,* *Turin. At that time, the Thames was the principal means of transportation in the city.*

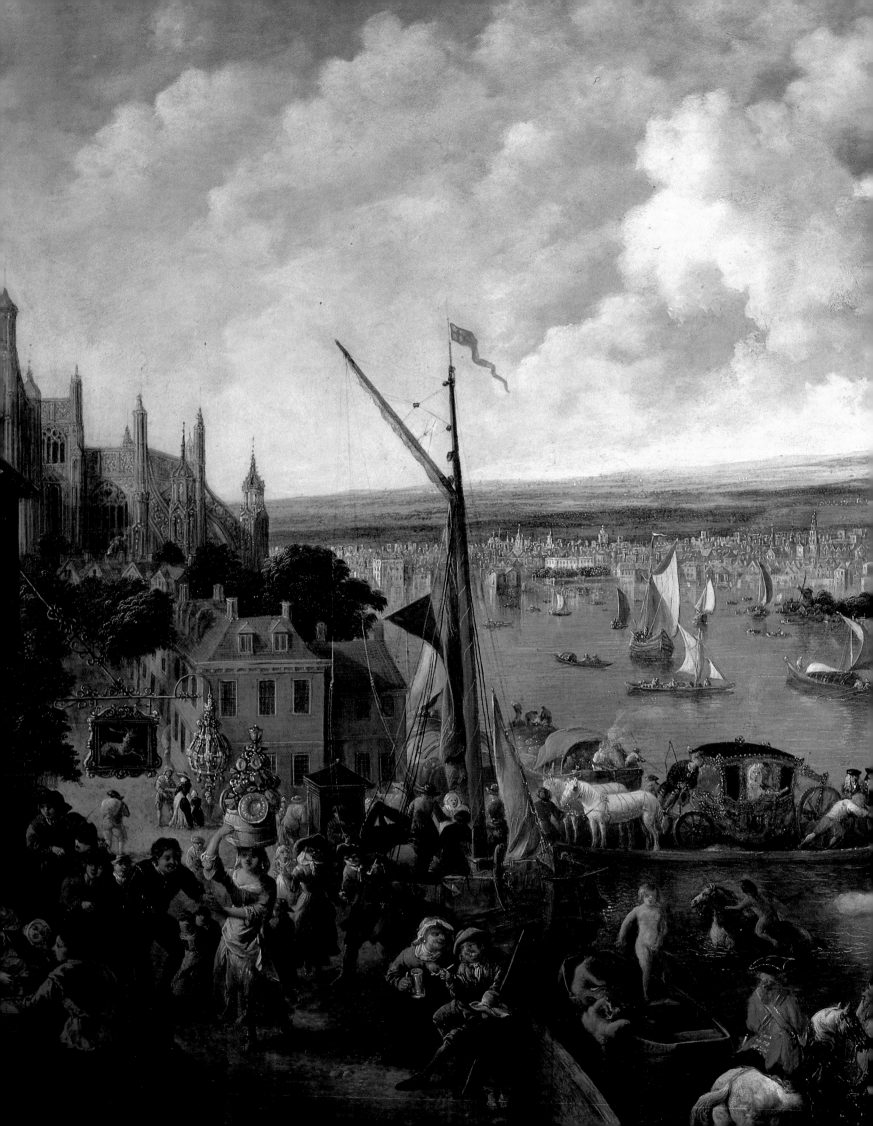

44 top
Victoria, in a photograph by Alex Bassano, became queen at just 18 years of age. During the early years of her reign, she was advised by Lord Melbourne. In 1890, the year of this portrait, Queen Victoria had been on the throne for 53 years; she was to remain there until 1901. An energetic, strong-willed woman, observant of conventions, she was deeply devoted to her husband, Albert of Saxe-Coburg-Gotha, with whom she had nine children.

44 bottom
With Queen Victoria's support, Benjamin Disraeli, the leader of the Tories, succeeded in passing an electoral reform that established the right to vote for all householders and £10 rent payers in the cities, thus doubling the numbers of voters. Disraeli, who was also a respected writer, polemicist, and satirist, worked to improve the conditions of the working class, taking an interest in public health and the right to strike.

44 center
In this painting by David Roberts, Queen Victoria arrives at the ceremony of the opening of Parliament. The scene is repeated, with few changes, in the present day: The queen travels to Westminster in a ceremonial carriage, escorted along the Mall by the Royal Cavalry.

The London of Queen Victoria, who reigned from 1837 to 1901, showed all the signs of a community that had grown too fast. Charles Dickens denounced the inhumane conditions in the orphanages, prisons, and workhouses, and his works accelerated the adoption of measures to defend the weaker members of society. Pollution also contributed to a worsening of conditions, and London's air was thick with the smoke from factories, workshops, and domestic chimneys. A dense smog is described by Dickens in one of the most celebrated passages in *Bleak House*. During this period, many other writers, artists, and politicians took up London's cause ("Jaws of hell, monster, metropolis of the empire" wrote Cobbett in 1821). In 1854, for example, Benjamin Disraeli published the novel *Sybil, or the Two Nations,* in which he spoke of the gulf between the worlds of the rich and the poor.

Late in the 19th century, Ebenezer Howard's name was indelibly linked with a new direction in town planning: garden cities. Taking advantage of new transportation systems, Londoners were encouraged to emigrate beyond the smog and the sprawl of offices, houses, and factories and the mass of malcontent humanity.

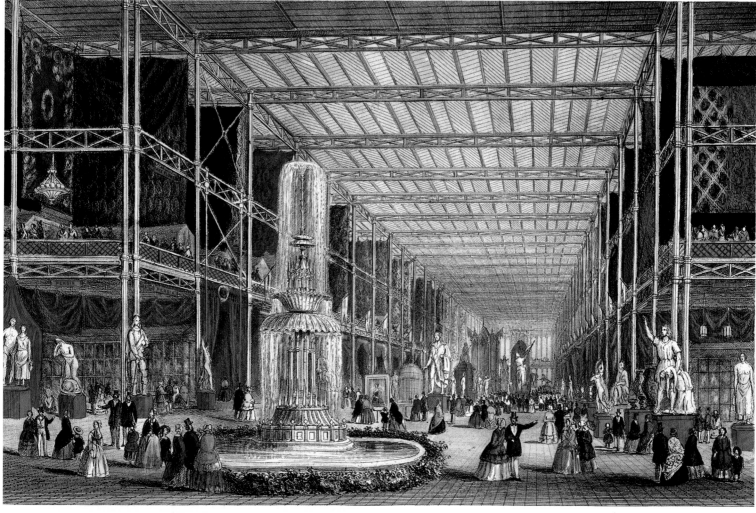

46 top
The old Westminster Bridge dated from 1749 and was replaced in 1862 by a structure designed by Thomas Page and Charles Barry. The bridge was one of the most evocative locations in the city.

46–47 The original site of the Royal Exchange, founded in 1565 by Sir Thomas Gresham, was in a courtyard where merchants bartered their goods, a tradition for a city that has been a center of trade since its founding.

47 top
This contemporary print shows a carriage passing the Coliseum at Regent's Park. This area was designed as an out-lying park with a number of villas and a palace for the prince regent.

47 center
Behind this severe neoclassical facade lies London University.

47 bottom
In the 17th century, Leicester Square was one of the most fashionable areas of London; in the 19th century,

it became known for its clubs and places of entertainment; and in the 20th century, it is still central to the capital's lively nightlife.

48 *A delightful cross-section of 19th-century London life. Heavy carriage traffic animates the street flanking the* *Central Post Office, and in the background, the moon illuminates the dome of St. Paul's.*

49 *The customshouses
of London's docks
served one of the
country's busiest ports.
The city's trading
vocation led, over
the course of the
centuries, to the*
*construction of great
warehouses, which
today are being
transformed into
apartments as part of
a massive rebuilding
scheme.*

50 top
The coronation of Edward VII, the successor to Queen Victoria, took place in 1901 at Westminster Abbey. This

contemporary photograph shows the hussars waiting for the arrival of the king. Edward came to the throne late in life, after the long

reign of his austere mother, who kept him away from state affairs by involving him in a series of long foreign trips and social duties.

In 1901, London's population numbered about 5 million. The suburbs, composed of thousands of single-family terraced dwellings with tiny backyards or gardens, extended almost endlessly. The demand for housing led the city center to be neglected, and it remained practically unchanged up until the end of World War II. The city's intense traffic was partly absorbed by the underground railways, which were electrified in 1890 and linked to the surface network.

London was no longer a city in the usual sense of the term, but as the geographer Geddes said, it had become a "conurbation," a collection of radically different urban centers linked by a web of metropolitan trains, buses, and taxis. The decentralization of industry removed the factories and workshops to peripheral areas where overheads were lower. The problem of housing was tackled through a combination of private (the Peabody and Guinness trusts, for

example) and public financing. The London of the early 20th century was also home to a number of great literary and cultural figures, including Virginia Woolf, the fulcrum of the Bloomsbury group; E. M. Forster; T. S. Eliot; William Auden; and art critic Roger Fry.

After centuries of splendid isolation, political events and the war on the continent obliged Great Britain to reassess its position, as alternative markets such as New York began to replace London at the head of world trade. At the same time, the British government was faced with the dominions' growing thirst for independence. The great London, the center of the world, was experiencing

one of the most difficult periods in its history: Mass unemployment followed the depression of 1929, when 3 million people were left without work throughout the country; traditional industries such as coal mining had declined; and much of Ireland was now independent. In the aftermath of World War II, the city was left facing an even more urgent problem: reconstruction.

52 top and center
Tower Bridge in flames (top), St. Paul's Cathedral (top left), and the Houses of Parliament (right) were involved in the heavy Luftwaffe bombing of June 1941. A total of 29,000 people were killed by the bombs, and the appearance of London was changed forever.

52 bottom left
Sir Winston Churchill visiting the city after the bombing of September 1940; in the June of the same year, Churchill had been named as prime minister in place of Chamberlain.

The public saw Churchill as a strong, determined figure capable of standing up to the Nazi threat. In fact, having abandoned his initial position of tolerance toward Mussolini's Fascist Italy, and

aware of the danger represented by Hitler's Third Reich, Churchill had promised to rearm Great Britain and established close alliances with the United States and the Soviet Union.

In 1944, the Plan for the London Region (which was integrated 20 years later with the Greater London Development Plan) attempted to impose a rational structure on the city's future development. The devastation caused by the German bombing campaign was only one of the problems facing the authorities charged with the task of determining the direction in which this immense urban agglomeration was to move. It appeared of fundamental importance to establish a green belt and to decentralize as much as possible in favor of the satellite communities built around the principal hub in open countryside. In the city center, reconstruction of the damaged buildings, the road network, and public spaces continued. One structure built at the time successfully merged old and new and won almost unanimous approval: Covent Garden, a redeveloped area in the heart of London, allows people to see a show, eat, shop, and meet each other in an attractive urban environment.

53 bottom left
The Coronation Coach, built in 1762 to the design of the architect William Chambers, carrying Queen Elizabeth II back to Buckingham Palace after the ceremony at Westminster Abbey. It was June 2, 1953, and the new queen was just 27 years old and had been on the throne for 16 months following the death of her father, George VI.

53 top left
Sir Winston Churchill during the 1945 electoral campaign. Victory in World War II failed to guarantee political *success for Churchill in the post-war years. But the great statesman did not retire from public life and continued to act as the leader of the* *opposition. He also devoted himself to writing, and his historical works earned him the 1953 Nobel Prize for literature.*

53 right
The queen and the prince consort, Philip Duke of Edinburgh, saluting her subjects from the balcony at Buckingham Palace. *The queen is wearing the Imperial State Crown, which contains 2,800 diamonds as well as other jewels.*

54 *Three symbols of the 1960s: the Beatles (top, in a scene from the film* A Hard Day's Night, *1964); Mary Quant, the woman who officially "invented" the miniskirt (center, during the presentation of a collection of shoes in 1967); and Carnaby Street, the street of fashion and excess par excellence (bottom).*

During the 1960s, after decades of indifference, London was once again the focus of world attention. Fashion, music, and rebellious youth took center stage. The songs of the Beatles and the Rolling Stones swept away the traditional melodies; Mary Quant's miniskirts were a scandal eventually adopted by the majority of women; hair was worn longer; and marijuana began to sprout in London's flowerpots.

As a result of the adoption of English as the international lingua franca, hundreds of schools sprang up in London to meet the needs of students from all over the world. Every part of Great Britain was affected by this particular boom, but London is the undisputed center, *the* place to study for 18- to 25-year-olds.

In the late 1970s, the hippies were replaced by the punks, a cult that has survived into the 1990s.

55 *Punks at Covent Garden. The punks are an established part of the London landscape. The colored crests, ripped and studded clothes, and heavy makeup unite youngsters of different social origins but predominantly from the most impoverished classes. The "movement" that developed in London in the 1970s spread throughout Europe.*

Today, London is an immense city, a melting pot of languages, races, traditions, and religions. A place where you can converse in English or any other language, from Chinese to Italian. In its 2,000-year history, London has expanded far beyond the confines of old Londinium and has become a crucible of races and myriad lifestyles.

T

he choice of where to start exploring a city is so important: The first impression can inspire eternal love or implacable hatred for a place. This is especially true of London, a city that may be as green as Hyde Park or as dark as Victoria Station, as solemn as the Houses of Parliament or as turbulent as a painting by Turner, imperial or plebeian. Some visitors elect to start their visit with a trip to the statue of Peter Pan in Kensington Gardens; others rush to the National Gallery; the incurable 1960s romantics search Carnaby Street for traces of Mary Quant; intellectuals browse the bookshops of Charing Cross Road; sophisticates yearn after a

Bond Street wardrobe; and society wannabees dream of meeting a member of the British royal family.

A wonderful place to begin a tour of London is a museum that many miss because it is overshadowed by many other museums. This museum also suffers from its location in the Barbican Centre. The Museum of London is, however, in the heart of the City, in the area in which London was born. From AD 43, when the Romans occupied the island, London and the City have been one and the same. Subsequent phases of history, the great fires, and the Luftwaffe bombing during World War II erased many outward traces of the Roman city, but the Museum of London exhibits what has been discovered over the course of the centuries and reconstructs tragic and glorious temples. Museum exhibits include the statues that once graced a temple dedicated to Mithras, a Roman mosaic, the Cheapside workshops, and a reconstruction of the court of Elizabeth I. This museum teaches visitors about the formation of a city, from *castrum* to trading hub to imperial capital, all of which is good preparation for exploring modern London.

56 *The Houses of Parliament are overlooked by a massive tower with four clock faces, erroneously thought of as Big Ben. The clock faces have diameters of 23 feet and the copper minute hands are 14 feet long.*

56–57 *The simple, square-cut lines of the Palace of Westminster are decorated with spires, turrets, mullioned windows, statues, and stone carvings. The building, home to the upper and lower houses, covers an area of almost 10 acres and contains 1,100 rooms and 11 courtyards. The complex contains meeting and debating rooms, libraries, the offices of the politicians and their assistants, and dining rooms. The interior is characterized by carved wooden paneling, arched passageways, and statues.*

57 top left
The last rays of the setting sun disappear behind the Gothic Revival spires of the Houses of Parliament, designed by Victorian architect Sir Charles Barry.

57 top right
The imposing Victoria Tower looms above the dark waters of the Thames.

58 top right

The Bank of England (this photograph shows the neoclassical facade designed by Sir John Soane) was founded in 1694 to finance a war against the Dutch. At that time, it employed 19 people.

Its early years were not particularly distinguished, and in 1731 it was discovered that one of the directors, Humphrey Morice, had embezzled the then-enormous sum of £29,000.

59 *One of the few City bankers reluctant to change any detail of his official "uniform": bowler hat, stiff collar, and a carnation in his buttonhole. Today, most bankers prefer a more relaxed look.*

58 top left

The Strand links the West End and the City. This street was once the favorite meeting place of Victorian dandies. Not far away is the official center of London, from which distances to other cities are measured. The spot is marked by a brass plaque.

58 bottom left

The site on which the present-day Leadenhall Market stands, in the heart of the City, has always been devoted to the food trade. The current building, designed by Sir Horace Jones in 1881, is particularly busy in the period before Christmas, when the displays are filled with every imaginable delicacy, both local and exotic.

The City, the area many associate with banks and insurance houses, is a self-contained miniature kingdom, with its own laws and hierarchies, a square mile with a population that at dusk falls from 350,000 to no more than 6,000. Today, gentlemen with bowler hats and umbrellas are being replaced by numbers of young bankers with the look of future millionaires. The moving spirit of the City is, however, still commerce. The Lord Mayor parades through his purely nominal realm once a year (in November) according to a ritual established in 1215, to pay homage to the head of the British magistrature, with all the pomp and ceremony befitting an "almost absolute sovereign." The costumes, the carriages, the plumes of horses pass the symbols of imperial power: law and finance.

The Law Courts are one of London's most characteristic sights. Bewigged and formally dressed, British judges continue to administer the law. Not far from the civil courts, the Central Criminal Court, better known as the Old Bailey, occupies the land that once housed Newgate Prison, infamous for the inhumane conditions in which prisoners were kept and immortalized by Dickens. The Inns of Court are populated with judges and barristers with their famous white wigs and law students from Temple Inn. According to an ancient tradition, the students are required to have dined at least 24 times at Inn's Hall before they are allowed to practice their profession. Temple Bar, which memorializes one of the eight gates that once gave access to the City, is now the city's official, ceremonial entrance.

Beyond Fleet Street, the traditional home of British journalism, the street names evoke the trades that for centuries dominated the area. In Cannon Street, visitors may no longer be able to haggle over the price of wicks for candles ("Cannon" is derived from "candlestick"), poultry, or garlic, but the ancient Livery Companies, the craftsmens' and merchants' guilds, still exert a certain influence over the administration of the City. Some of the most sumptuous buildings in the City belong to the surviving Livery Companies. Goldsmiths Hall, for example, where precious metals are certified, is in Foster Lane.

Financial power is concentrated in this corner of London. Young bankers, the heirs to the traditional frock-coated bankers, throng the area containing the bank, the Stock Exchange, and the imposing, dramatic new headquarters of Lloyd's of London, the world's largest insurance group, celebrated for insuring anything against any risk, from ships to the shapely forms of leading ladies. Had it have been active in 1666, Lloyd's might have been London's insurance carrier when, early in September, much of the city was destroyed by the Great Fire, the worst fire in its history.

The Monument, the tall Doric column designed by Sir Christopher Wren, the official architect of the London, is a memorial to fire, which, however grave in material terms, miraculously cost very few lives. The height of the column supposedly equals the distance that separates it from the bakery in Pudding Lane, where the fire broke out. The summit of the monument offers a wonderful panorama of the City, a constantly changing view that takes in two buildings that inspire equal amounts of love and hate among Londoners.

The Barbican deserves a good deal of the abuse that is heaped upon it. The British dislike the Barbican for many reasons: It has too much concrete, something that the British have never liked; it took 20 years to build; it is so complex and labyrinthine that it takes an age to learn its layout; and it is a symbol of the failure to attract new inhabitants to the depopulated City, and failures are never popular. Despite its many drawbacks, the Barbican is a wonderful place for lovers of classical theater and music because it houses the Royal Shakespeare Company and the concert hall of the London Symphony Orchestra as well as restaurants, movie theaters, and cafés.

60 left
In 1962, the Barbican Centre replaced a series of buildings demolished by German bombs during World War II. The center houses two theaters, a concert hall, movie theaters, art galleries, conference and temporary exhibition halls, a library, and the Guildhall School of Music.

60 top right
A glass of champagne downed at the bar: times have changed in the City.

60–61 *The Royal Exchange faces a City square that also houses the Bank of England and Mansion House, the official residence of the Lord Mayor. The city's first public toilets were opened in front of the Royal Exchange in 1855.*

61 top *A view of the City. Today, it is difficult to recognize the original nucleus of London that developed when London Bridge was still the only Thames crossing and the Roman walls still surrounded and protected the strategically important settlement.*

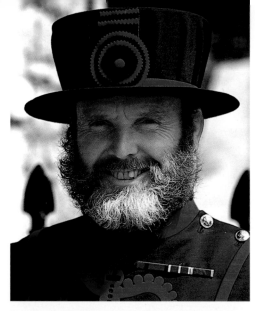

62 top left
In 1092, the year of its inauguration, the White Tower was the tallest building in the city, its battlements reaching a height of 96 feet. The tower houses St. John's chapel, which was built from stone imported from France.

62 top right
The Beefeaters are members of the guard corps of the Tower of London. The 42 volunteers live and work on the site where William the Conqueror confirmed the Norman domination of the island.

62–63 *The Tower of London from above. The two turrets at the bottom right mark the main entrance, and the large turret on the West Wall is the Beauchamp Tower, which housed illustrious prisoners. Behind the White Tower is the Jewel House, where the Crown Jewels are kept.*

63 top
Although the Globe Royal is hollow inside it weighs almost 3 pounds. The orb is studded with gems and topped with a cross and is a symbol of the universal power of Christ. The double band of pearls is set with rubies, emeralds, and sapphires, each surrounded by diamonds. The globe is used during the British sovereigns' coronation ceremony, together with the three swords of justice (representing mercy and spiritual and temporal justice) and the crossed sceptre set with one of the most fantastic diamonds of all time, the Star of Africa: 530 carats of pure light.

63 bottom
The Imperial State Crown was created in 1837 for Queen Victoria's coronation. Other crowns are also kept in the Tower of London, along with solid gold dinner services, antique weapons, and ceremonial jewelry. These unique objects are literally priceless. Elizabeth II's private jewels were, on the other hand, valued a few years ago at £300 million.

The British love Tower of London as much as they dislike the Barbican. The tower is a monument that every Londoner born within the sound of Bow Bells considers to be at least in part his or her very own. Nothing now remains of the original wooden edifice constructed by William the Conqueror in 1066 within the Roman city walls, but the White Tower from 1078 stands in the center of a complex that has witnessed great episodes in British history. The legends associated with the site are myriad, and there are ghosts by the dozen: Thomas Beckett, Anne Boleyn, and Guy Fawkes walk the turrets and walls but have apparently very little effect on the impassable Yeoman Warders, the Tudor-costumed guards known as Beefeaters (because they once enjoyed a right to a daily ration of meat).

The tower houses what can be considered as the oldest church in London, the Norman Chapel of St. John, as well as the royal collections of ancient arms and armour and the fabulous Crown Jewels. The jewels date from 1660, after the era of Cromwell, who had melted down many of the earlier pieces. The diamonds as large as hens' eggs, and the exotic jewelry can only be viewed from a distance. Visitors cannot linger: A moving walkway whisks the crowds rapidly past the crown of the Prince of Wales, the royal sceptre with the Star of Africa diamond (530 carats), the Queen Mother's crown, and the 109-carat Koh-i-Noor diamond.

The Tower of London, which at one time marked both the center and the boundary of the city, faces Tower Bridge, the most famous of the bridges over the Thames and the last before the sea. The bridge's Gothic Revival architecture and brilliant color scheme have made it a favorite subject for photographers, and until a few years ago, before the high walkways were closed in by glass panels, it was also one of the sites of choice for aspiring suicides.

A short distance away is the London dock area, which has undergone a massive and radical restoration program. Until a few years ago, the Isle of Dogs, the peninsula extending into the Thames, was a poor, working class area with no prospects. Today it is the center of a futuristic satellite town, a project that has aroused great controversy and has led to meteoric increases in housing prices and the destruction of an entire community. The workers have given way to the white-collar workers who inhabit old warehouses, now transformed into luxurious homes and office blocks of steel and concrete. Despite Prince Charles's protests that he did not like the idea of a forest of skyscrapers springing up alongside the docks, the Canary Wharf tower was built. The 800-foot building is the tallest in the city.

London Bridge is the oldest of the Thames crossings. It appears in songs and proverbs and has been here since Roman times. Various versions have been constructed in wood and then stone, been destroyed in fires, acted as the personal bridge of sovereigns, and even, in 1967, been sold brick by brick to a company in the United States.

66 top left
Although it would be difficult to imagine the building without them, the two massive bell towers of St. Paul's Cathedral were not part of Wren's original design. The architect added them in 1707; each was *designed to hold a clock. The portico also changed during the construction of the cathedral, which was originally designed with a single row rather than paired columns.*

Upstream along the Thames, back in the City, is St. Paul's Cathedral. The existing cathedral is actually the fifth church to be built on the site of a temple dedicated to Diana (its predecessors were a wooden and stone churches, a Saxon building, and a Norman cathedral). It was designed by Sir Christopher Wren, who, after the Great Fire of 1666, carefully eradicated all traces of the previous buildings—the last of which had been at least in part the work of Inigo Jones.

"Monumental" is the adjective that best describes Wren's St. Paul's, with its 356-foot-high dome, the Whispering Gallery that has delighted generations of visitors, and the funerary monuments of great figures in British history. Wren's building may not be inviting to its congregation and may not inspire sudden conversions, but Wren had quite different aims in mind when he designed St. Paul's. He wanted to erect a building that would stand as evidence of his genius over the centuries. The epitaph on his tomb—he was one of the first to be buried in the cathedral—leaves no doubt as to the opinion the architect had of himself: *Lector si monumentum requiris, circumspice* (Reader, if you seek his monument, look around you).

66 bottom left
St. Paul's Cathedral has been used for great state ceremonies, including the funeral of Sir Winston Churchill in 1965 and the marriage of Lady Diana Spencer and Prince Charles in 1981.

66 top right
The mosaics on the ceiling of the choir of St. Paul's, a celebration of gold-leaf and brilliant colors, were completed by William Richmond in 1890, long after the opening of the cathedral.

66 bottom right
The transept and the choir of St. Paul's. The cross-shaped plan of the cathedral ensures that all sight-lines converge in the center under the dome.

67 *The remarkable dome of St. Paul's from the inside. At 356 feet, the dome is the world's second largest; only St. Peter's in Rome is larger.*

68 top

*Admiral Horatio
Nelson scans the horizon
from his perch atop a
column in the center of
Trafalgar Square. The
column rises 160 feet,
and the statue is 10 feet
tall. The monument
was completed in 1842,
and it is said that prior
to the installation of the
statue, 14 builders
gathered to eat supper
on the top of the column.*

68 bottom

*One of the four
bronze lions by
Edward Landseer at
the base of Nelson's
Column. Because of
its centrality and
size, the square is
today the site of choice
for demonstrations
and New Year's Eve
celebrations.*

The route from the City, following the course of the river, to the seats of contemporary power is equally monumental. The Strand leads into Trafalgar Square, the site of mass protests and beer-fueled New Year's Eve celebrations, and the undisputed realm of tourists, pigeons, and Horatio Nelson, the admiral who defeated the French fleet at the Battle of Trafalgar. The column on which his statue stands is 160 feet tall, and the relief sculptures that decorate its base were cast from melted-down cannons taken from the ships defeated by the British fleet.

The square neoclassical facade of the National Gallery dominates Trafalgar Square. Many visitors find that because entrance is free, it is better to visit this museum more than once rather than risk overdosing on art. Illustrious art historians frequently offer lectures in the museum, but its is also pleasant to wander the galleries. Wonderful moments might include an afternoon dedicated to Rembrandt, a morning contemplating Monet, an entire day in front of the Leonardo cartoon, or perhaps an hour, but a profitable one, for the *Arnolfini Marriage* by Jan Van Eyck.

68–69 Trafalgar Square, London's most important piazza, was designed by John Nash and completed between 1830 and 1840. The occasion was the commemoration of Nelson's victory over the French fleet of Napoléon Bonaparte at Trafalgar in 1805. On the right is the facade of St. Martin-in-the-Fields, an important church because it houses the remains of great artists and because it served as a model for the churches in the United States. Designed by James Gibbs early in the 18th century, the church today hosts recitals of church music.

70 top left
Titian's Noli Me Tangere was hung in the National Gallery in 1856. The gallery has a number of works by the artist.

70 top right
Woman Bathing in the Stream is one of Rembrandt's best known masterpieces and is a portrait of his companion, Hendrickje Stoffels. The work was bequeathed to the gallery by Reverend Holwell Carr in 1831.

70 bottom right
Baptism of Christ was painted by Piero della Francesca for the Priory of St. John the Baptist at Sansepolcro. It subsequently passed through the hands of various private collectors and was purchased by the National Gallery in 1861.

70 bottom left
Young Woman Standing at a Virginal, by Jacob Vermeer. The National Gallery acquired the painting from an antiques market in 1892.

71 *Flemish masters are well represented in the National Gallery. One of the most famous works is Giovanni Arnolfini and His Wife, by Jan Van Eyck. The artist can be seen reflected in the convex mirror on the wall in the background, immediately above which is his signature. The painting was purchased in 1842.*

72–73 In 1870, Claude Monet stayed in London and painted this view of the Thames and Westminster. He visited the National Gallery—where today some of his best known works are to be found—but he does not appear to have been particularly impressed.

72 top
Cornfield and Cypress Trees *was painted by Vincent Van Gogh at St-Remy in 1889. It is part of the collection of modern art at the National Gallery.*

72 bottom
The Execution of the Emperor Maximillian *was painted by Edouard Manet between 1867 and 1868.*

73 Dancer with Castanets *is one of the most important works of the last phase of Pierre Auguste Renoir's career. This painting's companion piece,* Dancer with Drum, *is also in the National Gallery. Both paintings were purchased in 1961.*

The National Portrait Gallery displays portraits of the characters that have made British history great. Almost next door is the Church of St. Martin-in-the-Fields, the last resting place of illustrious artists, including Hogarth, Reynolds, and Chippendale, and the queen's parish church. Elizabeth II lives at the end of The Mall, beyond Admiralty Arch. The Mall is also home to the Queen Mother, who lives in Clarence House, and the arch recalls another sovereign, Queen Victoria, in whose memory it was constructed in 1910.

Buckingham Palace was designed by John Nash, and Queen Victoria was the first monarch to live in the building, to the great disapproval of the rest of the royal family. Despite the improvements that have been made over the years, the palace's 600 rooms are said to be remarkably uncomfortable. The queen and Prince Philip actually live in relatively small apartments, reserving the State Rooms for ceremonial occasions. The palace employs about 550 people in various service, management, and maintenance roles. Among them are the curators of the queen's art collections; a botanist; the keeper of the royal swans; the queen's two ladies-in-waiting; and a staff of 180 cooks, maids, confectioners, and gardeners under the orders of the master of the house. How the daily life of the palace is organized is not made public, although recently a number of employees have foregone their prestigious but modest palace salaries in favor of the

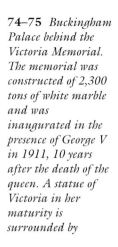

76 top
Motionless guards in line for the beginning of the most eagerly awaited ceremony of the year, Trooping the Colour.

76–77 *The broad expanse of Horse Guards Parade houses part of the Trooping the Colour ceremony: the moment in which the queen receives the salute from her*

soldiers. The various military corps parade in front of the sovereign before heading for Buckingham Palace. Horse Guards Parade is also the site of the offices of the Commander in Chief of the armed forces, and here, too, there is a Changing of the Guard ceremony at 11 every morning.

easy money offered by the tabloid press for tasty scoops. The ceremony of the Changing of the Guard is open to the public, as are the Queen's Gallery and the Royal Mews. The gallery houses part of the monarch's immense collection of art, and the mews contain some of the most beautiful historic carriages that on many official occasions are still preferred to the prestigious Rolls-Royce limousines. In addition, to raise the funds necessary to repair Windsor Castle, which was devastated by fire, the queen has opened certain parts of the palace to the public. There is no risk of bumping into Prince Charles, but visitors do get to see the Throne Room with its lavish velvets and gold stucco.

Such an idea would never have occurred to Queen Victoria, who is immortalized in an immense block of white marble in front of the palace. She reigned from 1837 to 1901, transforming in the process from the young girl depicted in a celebrated portrait by Franz Winterhalter to the opulent lady in widow's weeds, intransigent on questions of public and private morals, and still capable at 80 years of age of rapping the knuckles of her son, the future King Edward VII, an impenitent bon vivant.

The Mall's gates lead into St. James's Park, the oldest of London's parks, created by Henry VIII and beloved by all his successors. Once a royal hunting reserve, the park is still one of London's most elegant green areas and is at its best in spring. Swans, ducks, and geese wait for crumbs on the lake, and music can often be heard in the small bandstand.

English gardens can be found in nearby Green Park, an oasis of flowers and tranquillity in the heart of the city. This bucolic part of London has the highest density of ministries. Whitehall also houses the Admiralty and the offices of the head of M15, Her Majesty's espionage services, made famous by Ian Fleming's character James Bond.

Downing Street, home to the prime minister, is an almost anonymous city street. Until a few years ago, prior to the terrorist era, it was guarded by a lone policeman armed with just a truncheon, as a symbol of the fact that British democracy was part of the national heritage and political power had no reason to fear meeting its public. The area also contains the Cabinet War Rooms, Banqueting House with its nine fabulous Rubens panels, and a passage to New Scotland Yard, which until 1967 was the headquarters of the London police force.

The Horse Guards each day take part in the Changing of the Guard at Buckingham Palace. This is a favorite destination for tourists because they can admire not only the splendid animals but also the imperturbability of the cavalrymen, who are capable of remaining immobile even when assaulted by 1,000 massed camera flashes.

80 top

The Palace of Westminster was a royal residence until Henry VIII, who preferred Whitehall Palace, came to the throne. After its destruction in one of the numerous fires that have afflicted London over the centuries, the palace was rebuilt in the Gothic Revival style in the 19th century.

Further modifications and additions were necessary after World War II. The Houses of Parliament were badly damaged during the Blitz of 1940–41. The House of Commons was rebuilt to the designs of Sir Giles Scott, who copied the style preferred by Queen Victoria 100 years earlier.

80–81 *The Palace of Westminster from the Thames. The transfer of the seat of power from the City, the original nucleus of London, to the current site took place in the 11th century. The only part of the medieval building remaining is Westminster Hall, which dates from 1097 and has a beamed ceiling from the 14th century.*

81 top
The clocktower of the Palace of Westminster is 340 feet tall, and at night the illuminated dials are visible throughout the city. Over the years this has become one of the best known symbols of London, and the sound of Big Ben, the 14-ton bell, tolling the hours is used to announce the programs of the BBC,

the state television and radio network. Inside the tower is the No. 1 Room in which political agitators were locked. Among these was Emmeline Pankhurst, the ardent and combative English woman who, early in this century, led the movement demanding the right to vote for women.

81 bottom
The Houses of Parliament. The public is allowed to witness the sittings at certain times of the day, and British citizens have a right to speak to the member of parliament they elected.

Westminster is a veritable celebration of the Gothic and Gothic Revival styles. Parliament Square, created in the middle of the 19th century after an area of miserable hovels was demolished, is inhabited by statues of great statesmen; St. Margaret's Chapel, traditionally the parish church of the Members of the House of Commons; and Westminster Palace, which many centuries ago was the residence of various monarchs and since 1547 has been the home of the British parliament. Westminster Hall, the only remainig part of the original building, was built in the 11th century on the orders of William II and is closed to the public. The rest of the building was built in Gothic Revival style by Charles Barry and Augustus Pugin in the mid-19th century and restored after the destruction of World War II.

Westminster also has a famous clock tower. The chimes that during the last war announced the radio news broadcasts from the BBC are those of Big Ben, the 14-ton bell cast in 1858 and installed by Sir Benjamin Hall, from whom it takes its nickname. The tower also contains the celebrated No. 1 Room, the cell in which rabblerousers were detained. Here guards tried to calm the overheated spirit of Emmeline Pankhurst, the famous suffragette.

Nearby is Westminster Abbey, whose Gothic architecture is authentic. More than nine centuries have passed since Edward the Confessor gave orders for the construction of an abbey to begin on the site of an earlier Benedictine monastery. The good king had little time to benefit from his actions, dying just a week after the consecration of the abbey late in 1065. Edward the Confessor was the first monarch to be buried at Westminster. Subsequently, the abbey has become the traditional site for coronations and royal burials.

82 top left

This long row of coats of arms outside Westminster Abbey shows the extent to which the building has been linked with the history of the English Crown. From the times of Elizabeth I, Westminster Abbey has been an independent body answering directly to the sovereign.

82 top right

A statue of Oliver Cromwell in Westminster Abbey. A member of the minor provincial nobility, Cromwell the politician became the leading figure in the events that led to the execution of Charles I.

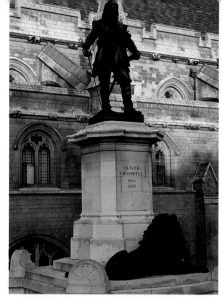

82-83 *Westminster Abbey's long history began in the middle of the 11th century, when Edward the Confessor decided to build a new church on the ruins of a Benedictine*

monastery. The good king barely survived to see its consecration. The first monarch to be crowned here was William the Conqueror in 1066, giving rise to a tradition that is still

observed. The last sovereign to be crowned in the abbey was Elizabeth II. Only two British monarchs were not crowned in the abbey: Edward V, the boy-king who is

supposed to have been murdered by his uncle, the future Richard III, in 1483, and Edward VIII who, prior to the ceremony, abdicated to marry Wallis Simpson in 1936.

83 *The towers of the west front of Westminster Abbey were added to the Gothic structure in the first half of the 18th century by Nicholas Hawksmoor.*

Today's building dates from the second half of the 13th century. Further modifications were made later, and the interior, in keeping with 18th-century tastes, was filled with funerary monuments to great poets, from Chaucer to Ben Jonson (who was buried standing upright) and Tennyson. Plaques commemorate Shakespeare, Shelley, Keats, T. S. Eliot, and Oscar Wilde. Major and minor figures in British history are also represented: David Livingstone; Gladstone; Issac Newton; Jonas Hanway, the first Londoner to use an umbrella; Elizabeth I; Mary Tudor; Mary Stuart; and Henry VII.

Westminster Abbey is a "Royal Peculiar," and it comes under a special jurisdiction and is directly controlled by the crown. The abbey is the London monument that best reflects the history of the realm.

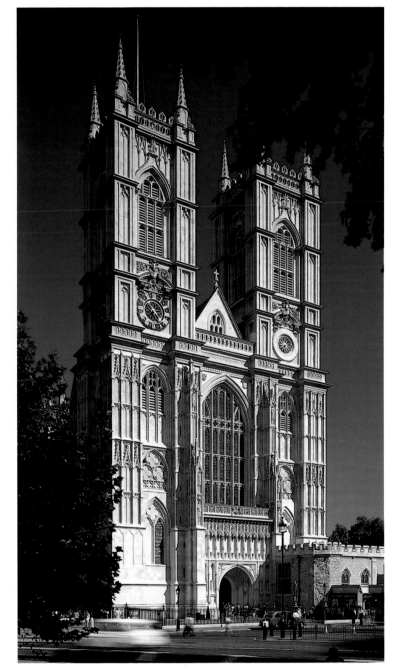

84 top
Stained-glass windows color the interior of Westminster Abbey. The abbey is famous for the number of illustrious figures buried here. The celebrated Poets' Corner was "inaugurated" with the erection of a memorial tomb to Geoffrey Chaucer in 1556, more than a century after his death. Ben Jonson was buried, according to his express wishes, standing upright, and other great writers, including Shakespeare, Keats, Kipling, and Oscar Wilde, are commemorated with plaques or sumptuous funerary monuments. Many political figures are buried here, including Gladstone, Chamberlain, and Attlee. The remains of Oliver Cromwell had a troubled history: Buried in the abbey, they were later exhumed during the period of the restoration.

84–85 *The central nave of the abbey is about 30 feet wide but more than 90 feet high. This gives the building an accentuated verticality. In the background is the screen separating the choir and the sanctuary. The abbey also contains a splendid cloister, site of the Undercroft Museum, a collection of effigies and sacred objects, and Westminster School, a prestigious private academy founded by Elizabeth I after the closure of the schools run by the religious orders.*

84 bottom
Another of the stained-glass windows in Westminster Abbey, which also contains the Grave of the Unknown Soldier, a memorial to Sir Winston Churchill, and the Warriors' Chapel, which is dedicated to the victims of all wars in all ages.

85 top
*The abbey's choir
contains the chapel of
Edward the Confessor
with his shrine, his
throne, and, until
recently, the Stone of
Scone, on which the
Scottish sovereigns
were crowned.*

86–87 *Westminster Cathedral is the most important Catholic church in London. It was built on the site of a prison at the end of the 19th century and was completed in 1903, to the designs of John Francis Bentley. The building's architectural style, an unusual blend of Byzantine and Renaissance, is accentuated by the external finish in stripes of red brick and white Portland stone. The belltower is 280 feet tall and contrasts strongly with the Gothic architecture of nearby Westminster Abbey. The cathedral is dedicated to the Precious Blood of Our Lord Jesus Christ.*

86 top and 87 *The interior of Westminster Cathedral is a triumph of marble. It has been calculated that it contains more than 100 different types from all over the world. The Byzantine influence is evident in the nave with its enormous green marble columns that recall those in the Church of Santa Sophia in Istanbul. The building was commissioned by Cardinal Henry Edward Manning, who intended it to be a memorial to Nicholas Patrick Wiseman, the first archbishop of the Catholic Church of England after the Anglican Reformation under Henry VIII. Among the works of art in the cathedral are the magnificent reliefs of the Stations of the Cross created by Eric Gill during World War I and a sculpture by Giacomo Manzù. The organ is also considered to be a masterpiece. The cathedral has fine accoustics and hosts popular summer concerts of sacred and classical music.*

89 *The collection of works by Turner (shown in the photograph is Crossing the Brook) is housed in the Clore Gallery, a new wing of the Tate Gallery. The gallery's collection is so vast that the paintings and sculptures are rotated through the gallery in shifts. Students and academics are permitted to visit the stores and admire the masterpieces that are waiting their turn to be placed in the public galleries.*

The Tate Gallery is virtually on the banks of the Thames. Sir Henry Tate, a philanthropist sugar tycoon, financed this art gallery, which was originally destined to house only British contemporary art but which has become a mecca for lovers of contemporary art in general. In the future, part of the collection will be transferred to the restored Bankside Power Station. The museums's Clore Gallery, a wing added to the main body of the Tate, contains the extraordinary paintings of William Turner, triumphs of light and raging elements. There are many museums away from the Thames, near Hyde Park.

88 top
The main entrance to the Tate Gallery faces the Thames. The gallery was constructed with the patronage of Sir Henry Tate, the sugar magnate.

88 center
One of the museum's neoclassical rooms leads into one of the world's most important collections of modern art. According to the intentions of the Tate Gallery's benefactor, the museum was to hold collections of exclusively British art, but subsequently the acquisitions policy was extended to include the most significant representatives of international painting and sculpture.

88 bottom
The Tate Gallery is unique, not only for the quality of the works of art on show, but also for the way in which they are presented.

90 *The interior of the Victoria and Albert Museum, in the heart of South Kensington, reflects the tastes of the period in which it was constructed. The fusion of influences ranging from Gothic to the Renaissance houses one of the broadest collections in* *London: Ceramics, textiles, silverware, and figurative art are all represented. The museum's most important collection, engravings and drawings, is housed in the Henry Cole Wing. The Print Room houses some 50,000 works.*

90–91 *Albert Hall houses an important concert hall. The building is dedicated to the prince consort, and the Greek-style friezes depict the triumphs of the arts and science. Prince Albert was distinguished by his patronage of and his enthusiasm for modern technology.*

91 top left *At Queen Victoria's behest, a memorial was erected in 1876 to her beloved consort, Prince Albert, who had died 15 years earlier. The structure is dedicated not only to the prince, but also* *to his great passion for scientific progress, and was completed in that Gothic Revival style that so appealed to the queen and that characterizes the "Museum Quarter."*

The Kensington district is devoted to Queen Victoria and her beloved consort, Albert. The prince is commemorated at Kensington Gardens by the Albert Memorial, a bizarre Gothic Revival folly and a paean to unrestrained kitsch. In front of the memorial stands another building constructed at the behest of Queen Victoria, the Royal Albert Hall. Although not blessed with exceptional acoustics, the hall is a symbol of the era in which it was built. Certain distinguished Londoners frequent the concert hall, enjoying a privilege that dates back more than 100 years and that is destined to endure: In 1863, whoever contributed £100 to the financing of the building project obtained the right of admission to the concerts for themselves and their heirs for 999 years.

91 top right
A skeleton of a Diplodocus *dinosaur welcomes visitors in the entrance hall of the Natural History Museum in South Kensington. The museum was built in 1881 by Alfred Waterhouse with the most modern techniques. The* *enormous halls offer an extraordinary survey of the wonders of nature, and the museum is a veritable citadel of science that includes an extensive geological section and an exceptional botanical reference collection containing dried leaves of all known plants.*

The museums in South Kensington make the area attractive to academics and children. In the Natural History Museum, a gigantic dinosaur stretching its neck out along the immense gallery opens a journey back through time to an era 65 million years ago, and the hall in which the effects of an earthquake are simulated unleashes cries of wonder and terror. Nearby, the Science Museum's interactive games involve visitors with technology and physics.

The Victoria and Albert Museum was officially created to display examples of "fine and applied arts," a broad agenda that is reflected by the variety of artifacts in the seven miles of halls and galleries. Highlights of the museum include the Constable collection, Raphael cartoons, the fashion gallery, furniture, the art of the goldsmiths, and Indian art. Anyone equipped with a letter of introduction confirming their academic good standing can use the library and handle rare manuscripts and drawings by celebrated artists. The Victoria and Albert Museum has something of interest for everybody, from the engagement ring of a Berber princess to the embroidered cushion of an abbess, from major works by Donatello to obscure Celtic crafts.

93 top
Richard Redgrave's
The Governess
*probably depicts the
life of a young woman
employed by
a wealthy 19th-
century London
family.*

Kensington Gardens, a very fashionable park during the reign of George II, fronts the nearby Kensington Palace. Some of the palace's rooms are open to the public, as is the Orangery, the beautiful conservatory built for Queen Anne early in the 18th century. The gardens also house the statue of Peter Pan, sculpted by Sir George Frampton in 1912. The children who at the turn of the century played with their hoops and sailed model boats on the Serpentine, the lake that unites Kensington Gardens with Hyde Park, inspired James Matthew Barrie to create the legendary character who decided never to grow up. Children continue to play on the perfect lawns and among the great trees in the gardens, as they do in Hyde Park, which, like all the major London parks, was once a royal hunting reserve.

Kensington Gardens' history is commemorated in the Rotten Row bridle-path, which links St. James's with Kensington Palace (the unusual name derives from the French phrase *route du roi*). Here each morning you can see the guards of the Household Cavalry heading to Buckingham Palace, part of a long-established ritual.

On Sunday mornings at Speaker's Corner, on the northeast tip of the park, near Marble Arch, anybody can express their views, be they doomsday preachers, political activists, or entertainers. The speakers attract crowds of onlookers, and there are often true debates.

Beyond Marble Arch, which was built in Serravezza Italian marble and was once located in front of Buckingham Palace, is Baker Street. The street was immortalized by Sir Arthur Conan Doyle, whose hero, Sherlock Holmes, resided at number 221B. The fact that the writer deliberately chose a nonexistent address has never discouraged fans of the great detective, and a museum displays the Victorian trappings Holmes and Doctor Watson used to outwit the forces of crime. The museum is true to the smallest details of the detective's life.

At the far end of Baker Street is Regent's Park. The park's lawns and trees are a sharp contrast to the blinding white of the Regency buildings designed by John Nash. Nash's work can be found in various parts of London, including Carlton House Terrace along the Mall, but this city park was the result of the megalomania of George, the Prince of Wales and regent in place of his father, George III of Hanover, from 1811 to 1820. The prince was attracted to the arts, and he like the idea of his name being linked with a style. With his protection and money, Nash completed in just a few years the extraordinary Sussex Terrace with its Corinthian capitals, the monumental Chester Terrace with a Doric facade, and Cumberland Terrace, a Renaissance-style courtyard. The whole complex was erected within what was once one of Henry VIII's hunting estates, a park that also houses London Zoo, and, during the summer, the performances of the Royal Shakespeare Company.

96–97 Hyde Park is east of Kensington Gardens, from which it is separated by the West Carriage Drive that runs from Alexandra Gate to Victoria Gate. The magnificent emerald green lawns make the park a favorite haunt, and Londoners come here to walk their dogs or perhaps to eat a picnic lunch. Hyde Park was once a royal hunting estate, and James I opened it to the public.

97 top Thanks to a law passed in 1872, anybody who has something to say can say it in the northwest corner of Hyde Park. Speakers' Corner is the platform of choice for dreamers, idealists, inventors, revolutionaries, religious fanatics, and materialists. At one time, public hangings were held here.

97 center St. James's Park is one of the capital's most attractive green areas. The severe Gothic Revival architecture of the Houses of Parliament (to the right) and the twin spires of Westminster Abbey (center) are both visible from the park.

97 bottom Rotten Row is a bridle path. It curious name derives from the French route du roi, because this road linked St. James's with Kensington Palace, which was where William III lived.

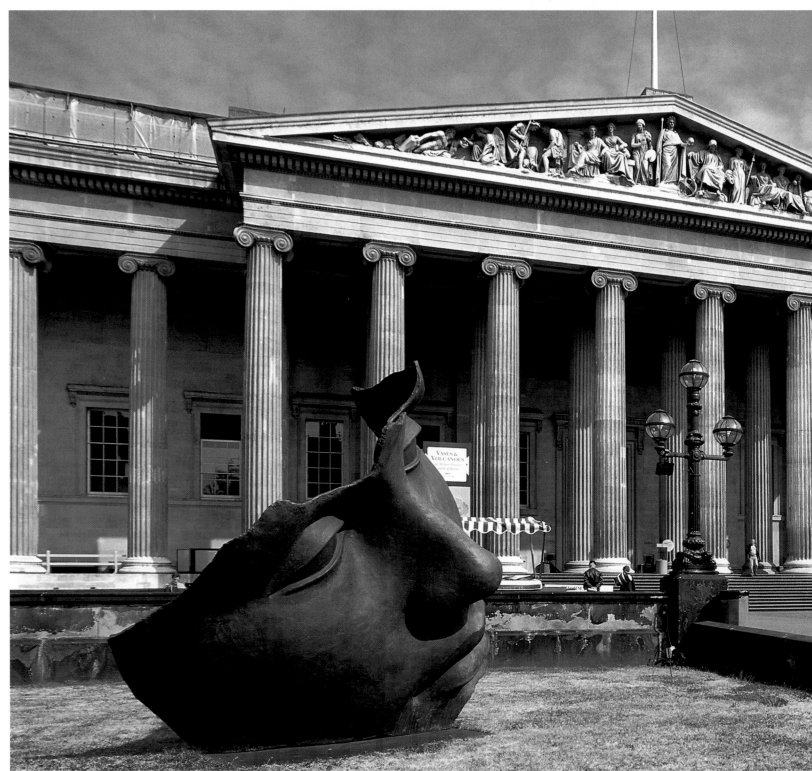

A very different atmosphere is to be found farther north. Virginia Woolf and the British Museum are two symbols of Bloomsbury, once so elegant as to be closed off with gates to keep out the hoi polloi. The area's discreet streets and spacious squares were the home of the Bloomsbury group, an informal set of writers, academics, and artists who lived and worked side by side. Virginia and Leonard Woolf, Edward Morgan Forster, Roger Fry, Lytton Strachey, and Clive Bell followed in the footsteps of other intellectuals who in the past had been attracted to the area by the presence of the British Museum, officially opened to the public in 1759 at Montague House, and by the University of London and the numerous bookshops.

Today, the British Museum houses one of the world's greatest collections. Most visitors tour the halls and corridors in a kind of bemused trance, stopping perhaps in front of the Rosetta Stone, the key to the understanding of hieroglyphs, the so-called Elgin Marbles from the Parthenon, or the Sumerian, Assyrian and Babylonian treasures. The museum also houses medieval, Oriental, and numismatic sections, and scholars can make use of the Reading Room, a domed circular hall that has accommodated the most illustrious figures in the realms of political thought, art, and literature.

100–101
The Egyptian section of the British Museum was part of the original bequest by Sir Hans Sloane. The

sculptures in Hall 25 began to reach London after the surrender of the French army in Egypt in 1801.

101 top
The Rosetta Stone is probably the most famous exhibit in the British Museum. This slab of basalt, found by a group of French soldiers during the Napoleonic expedition of 1799, is inscribed with a text in three languages: hieroglyphics, demotic, and Greek. In 1822, the scholar Champollion deciphered the text and opened the way to an understanding of hieroglyphics.

101 center
The great Hunts of Ashurbanipal, bas-relief friezes in alabaster, date from 600 BC and once

decorated the interior of the Assyrian king's palace at Nineveh. These were found in 1854 and immediately transferred to the British Museum.

101 bottom
The celebrated bust of Ramses II, today exhibited in the Egyptian Hall of the British Museum, was brought to England by Giovan Battista Belzoni.

102 top
The elegant Russell Hotel, facing the square of the same name, was opened in 1900. Finished in red terra-cotta, the hotel has an attractive Victorian atmosphere.

102–103 *Somerset House is a grandiose complex in the neonlassical style designed by William Chambers in the second half of the 18th century. On one side it faces the Thames and*

on the other the Strand. The building houses the Courtauld Institute, a small but sophisticated portrait gallery noted for its Impressionist and Post-Impressionist masterpieces.

103 top
Charing Cross Road is a name well known to bibliophiles: the best antiquarian booksellers in London are here. It is a pleasure to browse among the antique volumes, fragrant

with the dust of history. As well as antiquarian bookshops, central London is well served by many high-quality bookshops, such as Hatchards in Piccadilly (top right).

Covent Garden cannot be overlooked on even a brief tour of London. Once the kitchen garden of Westminster Abbey, the area has become something of a symbol of the city. Who knows if the duke of Bedford, when in 1630 he set about creating an Italian-style piazza surrounded by porticoes, could have had any idea of the success of his project in the centuries to come? Very little remains of the original structure, but Covent Garden is one of the focal points of London's social life. On one side stands the Royal Opera House, and on the site of the city's former wholesale fruit, vegetable and flower markets today is a plethora of stalls, shops, and boutiques. The complex is also known for its street entertainers, many of whom perform in front of the Church of St. Paul, which was designed by Inigo Jones and is known as the actors' church.

Another side of show business characterizes Soho in the heart of the West End. In the past, Soho was synonymous with vice and depravation. Even the least worldly of tourists had heard of the side streets and small squares in which you could find more or less anything from ladies of easy virtue to

porn shops, from fringe theaters to shops specializing in cinematic memorabilia.

Four centuries ago, Soho was open countryside, and the district's name derives from a hunting cry. Immigrants, especially French refugees from religious persecution, began to build houses and workshops, and in time the area began to attract artists, including Mozart, Verlaine, Oscar Wilde, and Dylan Thomas.

After the thorough "disinfestation" of the area demanded by a number of inhabitants, Soho now appears much more respectable, many of the more dubious clubs have disappeared, and visitors can safely browse the bookshops and exotic grocery stores. Bibliophiles head for Charing Cross Road, where there are countless specialist antiquarian and art bookshops. The miles of dusty shelves provide almost any rare volume, unusual title, autographed first edition, or precious manuscript. As evening approaches many visitors choose one of the West End theaters, one of the movie theaters in and around Leicester Square, or perhaps one of the myriad Indian, Italian, or Chinese restaurants that line Old Compton Street.

*Mayfair,
a Georgian district
considered to be
among the most
exclusive in London,
has elegant
residential buildings
facing Berkeley
Square.*

Mayfair has been synonymous with wealth, power, and unmistakably British class since the 18th century, when the area between Piccadilly, Oxford Street, Regent Street, and Park Lane became the city's fashionable quarter. The white facade of Regent Street was designed by John Nash for the Prince Regent and was intended to unite Regent's Park and Carlton House, the royal residence. Wide and opulent, Regent Street is crowded with luxury shops, such as Garrards, the queen's jeweller, charged with the maintenance of the Crown Jewels, and restaurants, including the Café Royal, frequented from the end of the 19th century by the city's most successful artists and still very much a place to be seen. Regent Street leads to Bond Street, Jermyn Street, and Burlington Arcade. That area is paradise for sophisticates and snobs who can buy their hats, shirts, and umbrellas from the same shops that serve Prince Philip and Prince Charles. Other visitors may prefer the Museum of Mankind, which contains the ethnographic collection of the British Museum, or the Royal Academy to catch the latest trends in contemporary art.

Sooner or later everyone stops in Piccadilly Circus. It is hard to understand the attraction of this cherub and his arrows. The statue is of the very Victorian Angel of Christian Charity, not of Eros as is commonly supposed. It is said that the angel's arrows indicate the location of a famous Elizabethan brothel. Peccadilloes continue to be committed in the surrounding pubs and clubs and even on the street corners. Some visitors choose this crossroads from which to begin their exploration of London. It may not be the center of the universe but it certainly makes a great starting point.

105 Regent Street was designed by John Nash early in the 19th century to allow the Prince Regent easy access to Regent's Park from Carlton House. The road begins at Waterloo Place, where it takes the name Lower Regent Street (in the photograph), and cuts diagonally through the center of the city.

106 *At the very center of Piccadilly Circus is a statue of an angel shooting his arrow. The small statue was erected in 1892 in memory of the earl of Shaftesbury and represents the Angel of Christian Charity. In Elizabethan times, the area had an* *unsavory reputation because of a very popular brothel, Piccadilla House. It must have been a fashionable locale if it gave its name not only to the surrounding area but also to an Elizabethan delicacy, the pickadil. In the late 20th* *century, Piccadilly Circus was known for huge neon signs advertising fast-food chains and electronics giants. Southeast of the area is the elegant St. James's area and to the northwest is Soho, London's peccadillo-quarter par excellence.* **107–110** *London at dusk from the former County Hall, facing the Thames a few yards from Westminster Bridge. In the background is the tower housing Big Ben and the Houses of Parliament.*

111 *The Haymarket, in the heart of London, links Piccadilly Circus with Pall Mall. This street is one of the focal points* *of the West End, with incessant traffic, lights, and crowds. The Haymarket houses the Theatre Royal, embellished with a John Nash* *portico (to the left in the photograph), and the Guinness World of Records, a museum devoted to incredible facts and figures of all kinds.*

113 top

In addition to the convulsive traffic of the metropolis, the lustre of its centuries of history, and its great monuments, London has a quiet,

more reflective side, especially in its outlying suburbs. This facet of the capital's dual personality is especially evident in its parks.

S ome years ago, a distinguished London gentleman earned his 15 minutes of fame for having walked all the streets of London. Visitors familiar with a London street map— not the British Tourist Board maps, which barely cover the City of London and the City of Westminster, but the Geographers' A to Z, with its index that runs from Abbess Close to Zoar Street—will recognize the enormity of his feat.

London is vast; its 590 square miles make it the largest city in Europe. It has a population of almost 7 million and welcomes more than 20 million tourists each year. The world's oldest underground railway network (the first trains were steam powered) carries 750 million passengers a year, and the surface routes carry 3 million passengers each day.

It comes as no real surprise, therefore, that, in contrast with the gentleman mentioned above, most visitors restrict themselves to the area within the Circle Line, the underground route that encloses the area of greatest historic and artistic interest. It would take months to explore even this relatively small portion of the city, especially for those who are not content simply to see Westminster Abbey and brush up their knowledge of the history of Greek art in the British Museum, but would prefer to at least dip their toes in London life.

For some time, local authorities have attempted to modernize the capital. British Telecom tried to replace its traditional red cast-iron telephone booths with tasteless, albeit vandal-proof booths. Having seen the error of their ways, they have now embellished the new booths with a form of cupola intended to make them easier on the eye for natives and tourists alike. The old red booths have been retained in "sensitive" areas of particular interest. In the same way, London's famous red double-decker buses have been flanked by more up-to-date models.

London Transport is very proud that all their buses carry the same logo; this does nothing of course to soften the blow. Similarly, tourists completing a pilgrimage to Carnaby

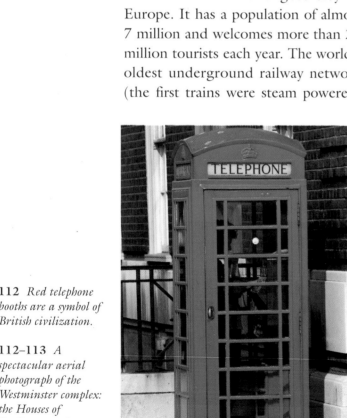

112 Red telephone booths are a symbol of British civilization.

112–113 A spectacular aerial photograph of the Westminster complex: the Houses of Parliament, the celebrated clock tower housing Big Ben, and the abbey.

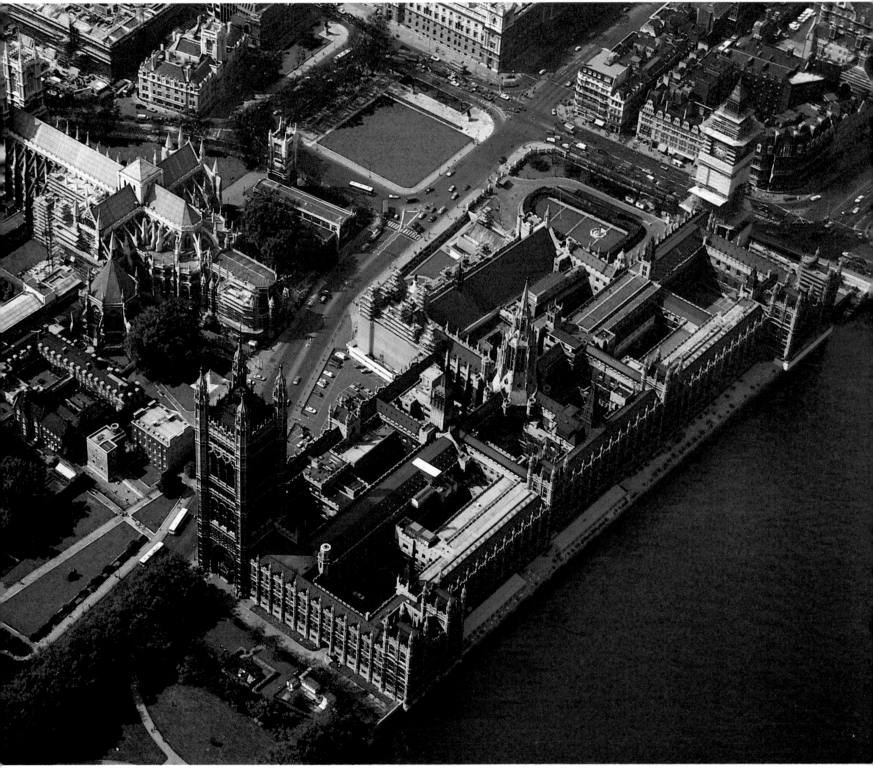

114 top left
Some of the carts that are used during the annual Parade of Beer Transport, a lively demonstration of bygone means of transportation.

114 top right
London bobbies are an institution. "Armed" only with a truncheon, a whistle, and a pair of handcuffs, they seem more akin to courteous and accommodating PR men than police officers and make a valuable contribution to the image of their city.

114–115 *The Mall, the avenue leading to Buckingham Palace, was created when the façade of the royal residence was rebuilt. In the background is the monument erected in memory of Queen Victoria in 1911. The avenue is particularly lively during ceremonial occasions.*

115 top
In London, a passing black cab will always remind you where you are.

Street in the hope of finding something of the spirit of Swinging London will probably break down in tears when faced with yet another shop selling T-shirts identical to those sold at home.

But all is not lost. London is so large and variegated that everyone can find his or her niche. Perhaps not on the first day or even in the first week, but sooner or later it happens. And in that instant, visitors forget the rush-hour crowds on the Tube, the omnipresent hamburgers of the fast-food joints, and the interminable lines for theater tickets.

London offers many wonderful discoveries: the royal swans were simply disguised geese in the story of Mary Poppins (the real story, not the Disney version), when the Keeper of the Pigs imagines himself in the role of a prince and the Keeper of the Geese in that of a princess. And if anyone invents a time machine, perhaps the best era to visit London would be early in the 20th century, when Bloomsbury housed Virginia Woolf, Roger Fry, Ezra Pound, luckless artists, idealists, and suffragettes. The Bloomsbury pilgrimage is obligatory for lovers of literature, who spend hours flicking through the latest publications or browsing among the secondhand books in Dillons, the immense bookshop facing Gower Street at the foot of an unusual and beautiful Gothic Revival building. Thackeray used Russell Square as the

home to the two friend and foe families, the Osbornes and the Sedleys, and Dickens lived in Doughty Street, not far from Macklenborough Square, where Virginia Woolf committed suicide in 1941. Long afternoons in the National Art Library of the Victoria and Albert Museum, consulting precious manuscripts, are another wonderful way to spend time in this city.

Presentation of a letter of introduction allows visitors to consult any document in the library's collection.

London fever can take an unbreakable grip at any time. Some travelers remember with gratitude the solicitude of the bobbies, the London policemen armed only with truncheons and a severe yet paternal expression. The Metropolitan Police force is a British institution as deeply rooted as afternoon tea and cucumber sandwiches. The police have no right to strike, do not earn very much, and frequently are obliged to tackle complex situations, but being a member of the force, created in 1829, is still an honor, and recompense is to be found in the gratitude of Londoners and tourists.

London has about 40 theaters in the central area alone and another 60 in the suburbs. The choice of performance is almost infinite: great musicals, Shakespearean productions, major West End performances, and alternative companies. Agatha Christie's *The Mousetrap* has been

115 bottom
Carnaby Street is a minor road between Oxford Street and Regent Street, but during the 1960s it was the symbol of Swinging London: even the austere Oxford English Dictionary *identified it with youthful, extravagant clothing. Thirty years later, the street has declined and is now a chaotic succession of shops selling tatty souvenirs and clothes.*

116 left
A visit to London would not be complete without an evening at the theater. Classic drama, new productions, musicals, and avant-garde works are all available. These night photographs show the facades of some of the West End theaters.

116 right
Along the Albert Embankment, in sight of Westminster Bridge, the old lamp-posts lend the scene a 19th-century air.

117 *"Official" London, the city of ministries, the corridors of power, and the home of politics, extends from Trafalgar Square to Westminster. All around, however, are the evocative lights of a city that enjoys its nightlife.*

playing continuously since 1952. Every evening in theaterland, as the area of the West End with the greatest concentration of theaters is known, curtains rise on the musicals of Andrew Lloyd Webber, the sophisticated comedies of Noël Coward, the light operas of Gilbert and Sulllivan, and Shakespearean tragedies.

The city's most important theater is the National Theatre, which is on the South Bank, rather than in the West End. Its first director, Laurence Olivier, immediately made his own classical mark, but today the National also puts on experimental works and has introduced some of the new stars of British drama, such as Peter Shaffer.

For those who can afford it, London is also a shopping mecca. Major stores are everywhere and everything can be bought anywhere, but only Harrods has the motto *Omnia omnibus ubique*: All things for all people, everywhere. Opened in 1849 by Henry Charles Harrod, the great department store is now owned by Egyptian financiers.

Visitors who do not want to buy anything, neither hat pins nor elephants (should you so desire, it could be arranged), can visit some of the departments as if they were museums. The Food Hall, for example, at Christmastime is full of hampers filled with every imaginable delicacy; the household goods department has table settings worthy of an emperor; and in the musical instrument department you can usually count on an improvised concert as potential clients try out the goods. The queen does her Christmas shopping here, and if after hours you see a Rolls-Royce drawing up at a discreet back door, it may well be the sovereign arriving to choose a gift for a friend.

Another institution for Londoners, and especially for bargain-hunting visitors, are the various markets. Every Saturday Portobello Market is overrun with shoppers examining porcelain,

120 top left
The fruit stalls from the old fruit and vegetable market at Covent Garden are still there, but now they sit side by side with well known boutiques, delicatessens, antiques dealers, and perfume sellers. Street artists are a permanent presence, an authentic tradition that was mentioned as early as 1662 by Samuel Pepys, who described a puppet show.

120 top right
Portobello Road has been home to one of the many London markets where shoppers can buy virtually anything, from silverware to old postcards, from lace to sewing machines. The 1970s were the golden age of this particular London institution in the Notting Hill area; today, because of its success and, above all, the hordes of tourists, prices have risen stratospherically, and visitors need a keen nose and highly developed bartering skills to come away with a bargain.

120–121 *Covent Garden has an evocative atmosphere; in the pubs, restaurants, streets, and shops, it seems as though time has been frozen at some point in the 19th century.*

121 top and center
Portobello Road is a paradise for collectors, who may well spend hours here haggling over a single item.

glassware, and teapots. A little of the Cockney spirit is still to be found in some of the less well known markets in Camden Town and Petticoat Lane. At the markets in Brick Lane in the East End and in Brixton, on the other hand, the atmosphere is decidedly exotic. A visit to these two city markets will educate any traveler unaware of the cosmopolitan nature of modern London: The first is an Indian enclave, the second, a little part of the Caribbean.

Anything and everything can be found at Covent Garden, halfway between an open-air theatre and a bazaar and a sight not to be missed. Covent Garden is perfectly placed in the city center, and it makes an ideal resting place between one monument and the next. The numerous stalls and small shops include one on the lower level selling perfect, ever-so English dollhouses, complete right down to the miniature silk roses to set in George III silver vases on an inlaid sideboard.

Another destination capable of triggering London fever is Kew Gardens, the Royal Botanical Gardens. This is just the place to understand why the British consider their countryside to be a park without rubbish bins. The greenhouses contain the

world's greatest collection of orchids and a titan, a huge tropical plant that produces an ugly and foul-smelling flower so rarely that the last flowering attracted thousands of visitors eager to photograph it. The herbarium contains 6 million examples, and 40,000 plants grow in the greenhouses and gardens. Kew Gardens is just one of London's many parks, but it is, justly so, one of the most popular.

The Thames, another must-see sight, is navigable downstream toward the sea or upstream toward Hampton Court. It can also be explored on foot via the 26 bridges that cross it within the boundaries of Greater London. Virginia Woolf wrote about the river's Great Freeze of 1608 in *Orlando*. In this passage, the writer describes how a 6- or 7-mile stretch of the river froze to a depth of about 20 feet and was brushed clear and decorated to resemble a park, with bowers, mazes, avenues, and refreshment kiosks. Near London Bridge was the wreck of a barge overloaded with apples, lying on the riverbed at the point where it had sunk the previous autumn. The old bargewoman who had been taking her apples to Surrey market sat, wrapped in shawls, with apples in her lap just as though she was serving a client.

121 bottom The Palm House in Kew Gardens, designed in 1840 by Decimus Burton. The suburban Royal Botanical Gardens were founded by Princess Augusta in 1759 and are renowned for their magnificent greenhouses.

Last but not least are London's pubs. The traditional pub atmosphere was described by P. G. Wodehouse in the Mulliner story in which the regulars knew each other not by name but by what they drank.

London's oldest pub, the Prospect of Whitby, in the Docklands area, has, unfortunately, been modernized. At one time, it was a den of adventurers, smugglers, thieves, and wrongdoers worthy of John Gay's *The Beggar's Opera*. Today, it is a chic bar where the suited members of the new East End development area drink champagne and eat lunch with a view of the Thames.

To find a real English pub, visitors should choose a pub at random, maybe one off the beaten tourist track, and claim it as their own. Initially newcomers will probably be treated with suspicion, and nobody will think of speaking to the intruder.

Then, one evening, someone will start a conversation like the one in the P.G. Wodehouse story: One beer drinker claims to remember when girls were six feet, two inches tall and

The signs of London's pubs are extremely imaginative: They celebrate saints, heroes, adventurers, and princes. Each pub claims to serve the best beer, at the right temperature.

boasted more curves than a coastal railway, and that they are now no more than five feet tall and disappear when seen from the side on.

A drinking companion agrees and adds that the same thing happens with dogs; one minute, the world being full of pugs and the next, there are only pekes and alsatians to be seen. A third drinker adds that the matter is all very strange and that we are probably destined never to know the cause.

If at this point, one manages to avoid thinking that the spirit of London really is an unfathomable mystery and also manages to avoid the error of interrupting, then perhaps something of this city has already found room in the heart.

124 right
The George Inn at Southwark is perhaps the most celebrated pub in London. It was built in the medieval style in 1676 and because of its historical value it is owned by the National Trust. It is the only pub in the city equipped with a gallery, and at one time it was also used as an open-air theater.

125 *Sherlock Holmes may be a literary character, but he has taken on the stature of a real-life hero. This pub pays him fitting tribute.*

126–127 *At one time women were banned from pubs. Today, this rule has been abolished but there are still rigid rules governing opening hours. Pubs may open from 11 in the morning to 11 at night on weekdays and from 12 to 3 and from 7 to 10:30 on Sundays. There are also strict laws about legal drinking age. Visitors cannot enter a pub and order "a beer." Light ale has little in common with barley wine, pale is not the same as brown ale. And while some may like the sweet flavor of shandy—a blend of lemonade and beer—others may prefer the sharper taste of a pint of old.*

128–129 *Parliament Street retains its solemn air in the evening. Political power has been at home in this area of London for at least 10 centuries, and while the statesmen may come and go and laws and governments may change, Westminster remains the same.*

130–131 *The London Bridge we see today was built in 1971. The site housed the city's first bridge, which was built by the Romans in the 1st century AD when they created their city and port here. Twenty centuries later, that small village has expanded into an immense city in which people of all races live together.*

INDEX

ILLUSTRATION CREDITS

Marcello Bertinetti / Archivio White Star: pages 8, 9 top, 10 top, 10–11, 11 top, 12–13, 14–15, 19 top and bottom, 57 top, 60 top, 62–63, 64, 65 bottom left, 75, 76, 77, 84, 84–85, 96 top, 96–97, 112, 113, 114 top left, 114–115, 115, 116 top right, 126–127, 128–129.

Angela Bertinetti / Archivio White Star: page 62 top right.

Luciano Ramires / Archivio White Star: pages 11 bottom, 55.

Giulio Veggi / Archivio White Star: pages 19 center, 58 center and bottom, 60 bottom, 61 top, 65 top and center left, 66 bottom left, 68 top, 74 top, 78 top, 79 top, 80 top, 81 top, 86, 87, 88, 90 left, 91 top right, 95 right, 97 bottom, 98, 99, 101 bottom, 102 top, 102–103, 104–105, 136.

Archivio White Star: pages 20 bottom, 46 top, 48, 49.

AKG Photo: pages 24–25, 24 top left, 27, 30–31, 34 center, 35 bottom right, 36 bottom, 37 bottom, 44 top, 51 top and center, 52 center left, 52 bottom, 53 top, 54 center, 70, 71.

Archivio Scala: pages 24 top right, 30 top left, 30 bottom, 31 top right, 41, 89, 92–93, 93 top.

Barnaby's Picutre Library: pages 21 top right, 36 top, 54 bottom, 58 top, 62 top left, 63.

Massimo Borchi / Atlantide: pages 16–17, 68 bottom, 103 top, 104 top, 116 top left, 117, 123 top right.

Camera Press / Agenzia Grazia Neri: page 13.

Collezione Privata: pages 20–21, 22 top right, 23 bottom left, 26 top right, 32, 34 bottom, 38, 39, 40 top.

Claudio Concina / Realy Easy Star: page 118 left.

Gian Carlo Costa / Agenzia Stradella: pages 22 top left, 28 center, 32–33, 34 top.

Marco Cristofori / Sie: page 65 top right.

Giovanni Dagli Orti: pages 25 bottom, 35 top, 42–43, 45 center, 100–101, 101 top and center.

Damm / Zefa: pages 107–110.

Peter Sanders Design: pages 18–19.

C.M. Dixon: pages 20 top, 21 top left.

E.T. Archive: pages 22 bottom, 25 top, 28 bottom, 30 top right, 40 center and bottom, 44 center, 52 top, 72–73.

Mary Evans Picture Library: pages 28 top, 29, 30 center, 33 top, 36 center, 44 bottom, 45 bottom, 50 bottom, 51 bottom.

Fototeca Storica Nazionale: pages 23 top and bottom right, 26 top left, 26 bottom, 31 top left, 37 top, 45 top, 50 top.

Cesare Gerolimetto: pages 12 top, 111, 119, 124 bottom.

Sylvain Grandadam: pages 1, 102 bottom, 114 top right, 122–123.

Dario Grimoldi / K & B News: pages 82 top right, 121 bottom.

Keystone / Sygma / Grazia Neri: page 53 bottom.

Massimo Mastrolillo / Sie: page 123 top left.

Simon McBridge / Agenzia Speranza: page 106.

Old Church Galleries: pages 46–47, 47.

Andrea Pistolesi: pages 9 bottom, 56, 56–57, 65 bottom right, 66 top left, 66 right, 67, 78–79, 79 bottom, 80–81, 82 top left, 82–83, 91 top left, 94 top, 94–95, 97 top and center, 105, 116 center and bottom left, 120, 121 top and center, 122, 130–131.

Retna Picutres / Grazia Neri: page 54 top.

Agenzia Luisa Ricciarini: pages 34 bottom left, 72 top and bottom, 92 bottom.

Ripani / Sime: pages 3–6, 60–61, 68–69, 74–75, 83, 90–91, 124 top, 125, 127.

Guido Alberto Rossi / The Image Bank: page 81 bottom.

Foto UBU / Agenzia Luisa Ricciarini: page 71.

Werner Forman Archive: page 85 top.